SEX AFTER SERVICE

SEX AFTER SERVICE

A Guide for Military Service Members, Veterans, and the People Who Love Them

Drew A. Helmer, MD, MS

ROWMAN & LITTLEFIELD
Lanham • Boulder • New York • London

Published by Rowman & Littlefield
A wholly owned subsidary of The Rowman & Littlefield Publishing Group, Inc.
4501 Forbes Boulevard, Suite 200, Lanham, Maryland 20706
www.rowman.com

Unit A, Whitacre Mews, 26–34 Stannary Street, London SE11 4AB, United Kingdom

British Library Cataloguing in Publication Information Available

Library of Congress Cataloging-in-Publication Data

Helmer, Drew A., 1970–
Sex after service : a guide for military service members, veterans, and the people who love them / Drew A. Helmer.
pages cm
Includes bibliographical references and index.
ISBN 978-1-4422-3056-9 (cloth : alk. paper)—ISBN 978-1-4422-3057-6 (electronic)
1. Sexual health. 2. Sexual disorders. 3. Soldiers—Health and hygiene. 4. Soldiers—Sexual behavior. 5. Veterans—Health and hygiene. 6. Veterans—Sexual behavior. I. Title.
RA788.H45 2014
613.9'508697—dc23
2014023952

Printed in the United States of America

This book is dedicated to the many veterans I've served through my medical practice. They say practice makes perfect, and working with dedicated men and women like you who sacrificed for me and my family motivates me to practice even harder. Thank you.

CONTENTS

Introduction   ix

1 What Is Sex?: Sexual Health and Function   1
2 Military Context and Culture   13
3 Effects of Combat Deployment on Health   25
4 Effects of Combat Deployment on Sexual Health and
   Function   45
5 Different Impact of Military Service on Men and Women   63
6 The Ups and Downs of Sexual Health   79
7 Am I Normal?   93
8 Let's Talk about Sex   113

Resources for Veterans with Sexual Health Concerns   137
Notes   145
Bibliography   151
Index   161

INTRODUCTION

Welcome, military service members, veterans, and the people who love them! This book serves as an authoritative resource on all manner of sexual health issues. Written for a general audience, the content of this book is based on well-accepted scientific theories and draws on clinical experience, expert opinion, and scientific evidence to share important information about sexual health.

Sexual health issues are common and diverse; more than one-third of Americans report difficulties with sexual function, and this proportion increases with age.[1] Common concerns include interpersonal relationships, difficulty engaging in sexual activity, physical abnormalities of the genitals and reproductive organs, and dissatisfaction with sexual activity. Numerous and various factors contribute to sexual dysfunction, including general health status, specific diseases and conditions, medications to treat some conditions, psychosocial dysfunction, physical and psychological trauma, and more. Sexual dysfunction has a negative impact on the overall health of the individual suffering with it and can also impact his or her partners and relationships. People want sexual health and want their relationship to reflect a healthy state.

Yet sexual health is a taboo topic. It is too often dismissed as unimportant and stigmatized in mainstream health care settings. In fact, sexual dysfunction is often not recognized, discussed, or appropriately evaluated. Patients report that they would like to speak to their health care providers about sexual health concerns but don't feel comfortable initiating the discussion, don't know how to adequately describe their symptoms, or feel they may be ignored or laughed at. Sexual health remains one of the more challenging topics for medical trainees, and even experienced health care providers often do not ask patients about their sexual health or function.

Military service members and veterans are perhaps particularly vulnerable to sexual dysfunction given some common experiences in the military and during combat deployments. Combat deployment is an inherently stressful experience, made worse with actual combat exposure and other physical and psychological hardships and trauma. This in turn contributes to higher rates of physical damage (including traumatic brain injury, amputations, and large-joint injuries), posttraumatic stress disorder (PTSD), and unhealthy coping mechanisms (alcohol and substance abuse). Medications commonly prescribed to treat or manage these conditions, such as opioids for pain and medications for PTSD, anxiety, and depression, can also contribute to sexual dysfunction. Perhaps worst of all, the most intense period of experiencing these complications of deployment is likely to occur when the service member or veteran is 20 to 35 years old, the life stage at which most Americans are dating, selecting a partner, and creating a family. Sexual dysfunction can have significant impacts on all of those important activities.

This book examines the effects of military and combat experience on sexual health and function in a comprehensive yet approachable way. It is based on a review of the science and informed by the author's experiences as a primary care provider and sexual health researcher. After treating hundreds of veterans as a primary care physician and as an expert in postdeployment health concerns, the author has helped veterans with a very wide range of sexual health concerns and variety of sexual dysfunction. He has seen firsthand how these issues affect the broader health and quality of life of the patient and his or her family. He shares these experiences by enlivening the text with illustrative examples that highlight the relevant points while protecting the identity of the actual patients.

After building reader knowledge and confidence in matters related to sexual health in the first chapters, the book describes what can go wrong for military service members and veterans. It then clarifies the boundaries of what is normal and what might be a sign of a problem requiring expert attention. Finally, it identifies appropriate sources of help and suggests a rubric for discussing sexual health concerns with professionals.

Starting with an introduction to the basic concepts of sexual health (chapter 1), the book establishes a shared knowledge base of pertinent biology, anatomy, and physiology with clear writing and organizational structure. By including a discussion of military culture, structure, and processes relevant to the sexual health of military personnel and veterans (chapter 2), the author lays the groundwork for the key lessons in chapters 3 to 5, the effects of combat on overall health, sexual health and function, and differences in these effects between men and women. These three chapters form the core of the book and delve into the factors contributing to sexual health and dysfunction.

Chapter 6 returns to a more general perspective, describing the effects of aging and life stage on sexual health and function. This content follows the discussion of effects of combat because most military service members join the military before the age of 20 and have a relatively limited history of sexual activity prior to military service. This chapter explores the overlap and interactions between normal aging and sexual health issues brought on by military (and combat) experience. Finally, chapters 7 and 8 clearly articulate a process for determining if there is a sexual health issue that rises to the level of a problem and what can be done about it. This is handled with a positive, hopeful tone and general yet effective suggestions on where and how to seek assistance.

ROLL CALL

To illustrate important concepts concretely, hypothetical vignettes and quotes are presented. Some of the case examples present events and outcomes that some readers may consider challenging. These are real issues experienced by veterans and service members but are edited to protect the privacy of the individuals. If you read the vignettes and think, "He's talking about me," you're both right and wrong. You are probably identifying with an experience shared by others as related in the vignette, but the details in these examples have been altered to ensure that they are not real.

By describing these complex situations empathically and in nonjudgmental terms, the reader can grasp the importance of the issues and glean the universal lessons even if he or she has not experienced the specific situation. Many of the characters recur throughout the book and have their relationships evolve with each appearance. Keep reading to see what happens to the character, particularly as he or she gets to the point of seeking help and resolving the issue by chapter 8. The following list introduces these characters with a brief synopsis.

- **David and his wife, Susan**: David suffered a catastrophic traumatic brain injury (TBI) in combat and is minimally responsive. He lives at home with his wife, Susan; their daughter; and around-the-clock support from paid caregivers.
- **Edward and his mother, Doris**: Edward, 22 years old, suffered a serious TBI in combat and lives with his mother. He has great difficulty getting around, using a walker and other prosthetic devices, but is able to think for himself.
- **Ted**: Ted lost his left leg and left arm in a blast injury and has recurrent bone infections in the stump of his left leg.
- **Clarissa, her parents, and her daughter**: Clarissa suffered complications of a back surgery after falling off a truck while deployed. She uses a motorized wheelchair due to persistent leg weakness and also has persistent urinary incontinence.
- **Juan and his mother**: Juan suffered a severe TBI with residual endocrine abnormalities. He lives in a group home and no longer is able to see his ex-wife or children.
- **Joe and his wife, Megan**: Joe had a moderate TBI during deployment and has continuing sexual dysfunction.
- **Maria, her boyfriend, and her sister**: Maria experienced recurrent sexual trauma while deployed and suffers from PTSD and depression.
- **Tom and his wife, Lisa**: Tom was deployed twice to Iraq. He is now a police officer who has PTSD with recurrent nightmares that he acts out while asleep. He was prescribed a selective serotonin reuptake inhibitor for his PTSD and experienced sexual side effects. He learned that his wife had an extramarital affair while he was deployed.

- **Julio**: Julio moved to a new city to start over after he separated from the military. He has PTSD and an alcohol problem that interfered with his plans.
- **Rhonda**: A former marine sergeant who discusses her experience as a woman during deployment.
- **Jonah**: A marine who shares his perceptions and experiences as a marine regarding sexual health.
- **Jack and his wife, Monica**: Jack suffers from chronic low back pain even after surgery and takes pain medicines for these problems. He shares the escapades of the guys in his unit at the forward operating base. Jack joined the military at 20 years old, deployed at 22 years old, and separated at 23 years old.
- **Laurie**: A recently retired officer in her fifties, she talks about menopause and being a woman in the military.
- **Steve**: A Vietnam veteran, Steve was married three times and is experiencing declining health now that he's in his sixties. He has experienced erectile dysfunction for a long time and has firm ideas about role expectations for men and women.
- **Connie and her husband, Doug**: A nurse with the Army Reserve who was deployed to the Gulf War in 1990–1991. She has had pain with vaginal sexual intercourse and a lack of climax or orgasm.
- **Mark**: A 37-year-old navy seaman with 19 years of service who has a wife, Mary, stateside but enjoys regular extramarital sexual activities while deployed abroad.
- **Eric**: A young, 18-year-old, new army recruit.

I chose to write a book about the sexual health of veterans because of these people. Although all the details are fictionalized, I worked with patients like these characters every day in a clinic where, as a general internal medicine doctor, I provide primary care services for adult men and women. Because I specialize in postdeployment health concerns, I would see men and women who had served their country in various different deployments, such as Vietnam, the Persian Gulf, Iraq, and Afghanistan, and come back from war "not the same." I've had the opportunity to explore with them why they might be different, including biological, psychological, social, and spiritual reasons. Many of these veterans had questions about their sexual health specifically, suffered with the impact of the sexual health issues, and yet didn't know what to do about them, how to get help with them, or even whether their health care providers would take them seriously. Of course, they had other problems, too, some of which fell more squarely in the realm of the health care system, but the sexual health issues were important to them and often their partners as well.

A series of observations about the sexual health of my veteran patients captured my attention. In my daily practice as a primary care physician, I realized that I was frequently prescribing phosphodiesterase-5 inhibitors (PDE5i), medicines for erectile dysfunction like sildenafil and vardenafil, to men in their twenties. They and I agreed that this was a problem that needed to be addressed more thoughtfully and comprehensively. We couldn't believe a pill was the solution. At the time, though, it seemed to me to be the only tool I had in my toolbox to help with any sexual health problem.

As I reached out to experts and listened more closely to my patients, I realized there were a whole variety of sexual health issues in my recently deployed veterans, some of general concern and others more specifically related to their military experience. I understood that while PDE5i were appropriate for some of these issues, there were other tools and experts that I could recommend and facilitate access for my patients. My growing knowledge and experience in the realm of sexual health concerns gave me more confidence to help my patients, and I began to ask all of them if they had any sexual health issues they wanted to discuss. In turn, this gave my patients greater opportunity to disclose their concerns and ask questions. They became more hopeful about getting assistance for their sexual health concerns, including the right care and management to help resolve the problems.

This book is a summary of the science of sexual health and my knowledge, gained through collaboration with my patients. It is written for them and other veterans and military personnel like them as well as the people who love them.

1

WHAT IS SEX?

Sexual Health and Function

Sexual health is contingent on many things, but most central is the person's overall health and function. Reproduction, the evolutionary driver of human sexual health, requires a certain level of general health to maintain ovulation and menses in women and sperm production in men. Sexual health is about much more than reproduction in modern societies, of course, and general health and function is also associated with its many other aspects.

Health is the most valuable thing a person can possess, but what is it? The World Health Organization (WHO) defines health as "a state of complete physical, mental, and social well-being and not merely the absence of disease or infirmity." Health is a state of homeostasis, or balance, which depends on a multitude of factors. Too much or too little of a particular activity or behavior can tip an individual into discomfort or even illness or disease, resulting in a diminished quality of life or unhappiness.[1]

For example, humans require adequate and appropriate nutrition to live and thrive—too little, and humans experience hunger, grow weak or sick, and eventually die. It's a balancing act, though, as too much food or the wrong type of food can cause immediate negative effects. Think of how some foods can lead to indigestion, diarrhea, or nausea, especially when eaten in excess. Over a longer term, too much food or unhealthy foods can contribute to obesity and shorten the life span through complications of obesity, such as diabetes, high blood pressure, heart attacks, and strokes.

Our bodies require the right balance of food, hydration, physical activity, social stimulation, and a multitude of other inputs to maintain health and optimize function. Achieving the right balance is an ever-present challenge.

Health is experienced differently for everyone. Health status, an individual's physical, mental, and social well-being at a certain point in time, depends on body structure and function, too. It seems obvious that an individual missing a limb has a different state of health compared to someone with all limbs intact because of the structural differences. The inherent ability to function and engage in life activities is different. Health can also be impaired if all the limbs are intact but for some reason the function of one is diminished. While one's health status is different, every individual's health can be optimized within the parameters determined by the different body structures and function.

Health is also contingent on the individual's surroundings. Depending on the environment, the optimal balance of the factors may change; what works well in one situation may be disastrous in another. Similarly, limitations of structure or function can be compensated for by modifications to the individual's setting or environment. Many prostheses and other devices have been developed to help people compensate for structural or functional abnormalities. Sometimes, the built environment—buildings, sidewalks, offices, and vehicles—can be modified to accommodate structural or functional deficits.[2]

Think of how a missing or poorly functioning hand can impact one's health. The ability of the individual to eat and take in nutrition might be affected, perhaps requiring more time to get enough food to the mouth. This activity may be especially messy, too, as the individual spills food off the fork while trying to get it to one's mouth. Given the importance of communal eating in modern American society, difficulty eating might change the individual's ability to interact with others socially in the context of a meal. Others may not want to witness the messy process of someone eating without a hand. Or the individual may not want others to be present due to a sense of embarrassment. The difficulties could be perceived as barriers to participation and produce secondary effects on health by contributing to withdrawal from social activities and promoting a sense of isolation. Using a prosthetic hand, employing different eating utensils, modifying food choices, or changing other aspects of the dining experience can overcome many of the challenges to eating presented by a missing hand. The individual's health can be optimized.

This comprehensive consideration of health is important to understanding the human condition. Sometimes called the biopsychosocial approach, it more completely captures the totality of what humans experience and value. In contrast, much of the training for health care professionals focuses on disease rather than health. This can result in a disproportionate attention to the biomedical aspects of health and biomedical solutions with a relative disregard for the context.

SEXUAL HEALTH AND FUNCTION

These same concepts of health and function apply to sexual health. The WHO helpfully extends the definition of overall health to define sexual health as "a state of complete physical, mental, and social well-being related to sexuality and not merely the absence of disease or infirmity." In fact, a biopsychosocial approach is especially critical to address sexual health.

Sexual health is a critical part of the human condition. Sexual health incorporates the individual's sexuality, or core identity related to sexual thoughts and activities, as well as several other concepts, including baseline desire, the sexual response cycle, and the mental and social aspects of engaging in sexual activity.

A core element of sexual health is the biological drive to reproduce, popularly called the sex drive. The desire to engage in sexual activity is a powerful, hardwired function in the human body that ensures the survival of the human species. Sexual activity can result in reproduction and lead to a baby—a new human being and a wonderful thing. But sexual health and sexuality are about more than just reproduction. We all create our own sexual identity—our sexuality—through our thoughts and actions. Sexuality incorporates everything about us and our behaviors that relates to sexual health and the ability to engage in erotic and related behaviors. Humans learn through their own trial and error and experiencing others' responses to their behaviors. They also apply various lessons from observing others' interactions and behaviors to optimize their opportunity to engage in sexual activity.

VOCABULARY

To ensure the most effective communication, this book will use standard terms to refer to sexual organs, activities, and related issues.[3] The following section provides a review of some basic terms relevant to sex, sexual health, and sexual function.

The male external genitals, or sex organs, consist of the penis and scrotum hanging down from the front of the body between the legs. The penis itself includes the glans, or head, at the end; the foreskin, or loose skin that covers the glans; and the shaft. Some men have the foreskin of the penis removed by a surgical procedure called circumcision. Often performed in the first days of life or at puberty, circumcision is done for religious, traditional, or hygiene reasons. The testicles, or testes, are the ball-like structures inside the scrotum. They make the sperm, which are the cells that join with the eggs from the women to form a new human being.

During ejaculation, the sperm are transported from the testes out of the penis via tubes called the vas deferens. As the sperm pass along these tubes, additional liquid is added by glands along the way, including the seminal vesicles and the prostate. The vas deferens joins the urethra, the tube from the bladder that allows urine to exit the penis.

The female genitals include the vulva on the outside of the front of the body between the legs, the clitoris in its hood at the upper aspect of the vulva, and the vagina, which is the pouch that opens into the woman's body through the vulva. The hymen is a skin-like covering that partially blocks the vagina prior to initial penetration. The ovaries, fallopian tubes, and uterus, with its opening called the cervix, are the internal reproductive organs in a woman.

The eggs are contained in the ovaries, and as they mature, they are released and transported through the fallopian tubes to the uterus. If the egg is fertilized by a man's sperm at that point, the tiny embryo may implant in the lining of the uterus. If not, the unfertilized egg and the lining will be shed as part of the monthly menses, or period.

There are other body structures and areas that are often engaged during sexual activity. These are areas of the body that are more sensitive, respond to stimulation, and can promote sexual arousal in both men and women. These erogenous zones include the lips, neck, breasts and nipples, the anus and the perineum (the area between the genitals and the anus), and the inner thighs. Stimulating these parts of the body is important to ensuring full arousal and can help to maintain interest and pleasure throughout sexual activity. Stimulation of these areas at the beginning of sexual activity, such as with kissing or stroking, is called foreplay and is an important precursor of more intense forms of sexual activity, such as penetrative intercourse.

While we may initially think of the genitals and erogenous zones when we think of sexual activity, the entire body is engaged in the sexual response. It is a complex systemwide set of processes and reactions that includes several parts of the nervous system, such as the brain and spinal cord; sensory input from the eyes, ears, nose, mouth, and skin (all five senses) via nerves; the autonomic nervous system, which controls things like breathing and blood vessel size; and the motor nerves, which control movement. The response also requires hormones circulating in the blood, glands in the reproductive organs and genitals that produce lubricating fluids and mucus, and the small blood vessels in the genitals and elsewhere.

And what is sex? For many, especially heterosexual individuals, sex implies the specific example of sexual activity in which the penis enters the vagina, or penetrative vaginal sexual intercourse. There are many other ways of achieving climax through physical stimulation, though. Some of the more common activities include oral sex in which one partner uses his or her mouth and tongue to stimulate the penis and scrotum (fellatio) or the vulva and clitoris (cunnilingus). Some couples engage in anal sex, which refers to the stimulation of the anus and perineum around it. This often implies penetration of the anus with the penis (or a surrogate, such as a dildo or similar object) but could also refer to stimulation of the anus with the tongue or fingers. Partners will also use their hands to stimulate each other's genitals; this has been called petting. Sodomy is the more general term used to describe oral or anal sex and is the term used in legal contexts. Masturbation describes self-stimulation, when a man or woman engages in activities to generate a sexual response in him- or herself either in private or in the presence of others.

HUMAN DEVELOPMENT OF THE SEX AND REPRODUCTIVE ORGANS

It is interesting to note that early in fetal development, the sex cannot be determined by visible differences in fetal body structure. By tracing development, one can see how different body structures in men and women are "related" in the sense that they are derived from the same protoplasm. By about the twelfth week in utero, male and female human fetal genitalia and reproductive organs have begun to visibly differentiate. Understanding the common origins of these body parts helps one understand the sexual response cycle and what can go wrong with sexual health.

For example, the clitoris in women and the glans penis in men come from analogous cell clusters in the fetus. That cluster of cells migrates to different locations on the male and female bodies and ends up looking quite different. They remain similar, though, in that both structures are among the most sensitive portions of the genitalia and have more nerve endings than most body surfaces. This high density of nerve endings enhances the importance of these structures in sexual activity and ensures their role in the sensory feedback during sexual intercourse.

The gonads are the cells that produce the core genetic material for potential offspring. These migrate and become the ovaries in women and testicles in men. These organs also produce sex hormones that contribute to the overall milieu in which reproductive and sexual behaviors occur.

The vagina in women and the shaft of the penis in men are analogous, derived from similar earlier fetal structures. Beyond the obvious inside/outside differences in the resultant body part, the innervation and presence of lubricating glands differentiates the male and female sex functions.

Further sexual development after birth, especially at puberty, contributes to the visible differences between men and women. The gonads mature and promote full reproductive capability with maturation of the testicles in men and ovaries, uterus, and breasts in women. The secondary sex characteristics, including breast development in women, facial and body hair, and changes in muscle mass and bone structure, also manifest and provide visible evidence of sexual differentiation.

In the brain as well, the hypothalamus and pituitary provide central regulation of the hormonal milieu and allow for communication between the periphery and brain cell activities. The differences between men and women in these hormone control centers begin early in life but become more prominent with puberty and maturation.

IS SEXUAL HEALTH IMPORTANT?

How important is sex? That depends on your perspective and situation. Sexual activity is not essential for an individual's life, of course, but it is required for continued existence of the human species. Our bodies are built and programmed to procreate. This includes hardwiring of the human body's nervous system (brain, spinal cord, and nerves), hormone system, and reproductive organs to identify opportunities for and to engage in sexual activity.

Some people choose to never engage in sexual activity or choose to stop engaging in sexual activity. Think of various religious orders requiring celibacy. This is not a unique phenomenon; examples of individuals publicly renouncing sexual relations while joining special organizations is almost universally present in diverse cultures and traditions around the world. Many of these individuals would say that they are happy and that their sexual health is optimized, but their motivations and rewards for forgoing sexual activity are likely quite complex. While universal in the diverse societies of the world, the number of individuals who choose to abstain from sex for these reasons is not very large relative to the entirety of humanity.

Some people don't have the opportunity to engage in sexual activity. Having intimate physical sexual relations with another person can depend on a number of environmental conditions beyond the control of the individuals. Even masturbation may similarly be constrained by societal expectations and living situations. People who can't engage in sexual activity may not be happy, and their sexual health may be suboptimal, but they don't die because of the lack of sexual activity.

Optimizing sexual health is important to most people. Sexual activity can be fun and contribute to other positive life experiences, like a strong, long-lasting partnership with another person. Of course, some sexual activity can result in babies, which is a desirable outcome for many people. On the other hand, sexual desires can be distracting and compel people to engage in unhealthy behaviors. Sometimes, poorly considered sexual activity can get you in trouble. We explore these ideas in the context of military personnel and veterans throughout this book.

BASELINE DESIRE, OR LIBIDO

Baseline desire, also called libido, is determined largely by the brain and systemic hormones. Everyone has a baseline level of desire, the degree to which they are interested in sexual activity. There is also the desire that "flares up" given particular situations and circumstances, discussed below as the first phase of the sexual response cycle.

The role of the reproductive hormones in baseline desire is very important in both men and women. Given the cyclical nature of women's menstrual cycle and the hormones controlling it, the importance for desire of various hormone levels, their relative balance, and the dynamic shifts in the levels and balance are better described in women than in men. Depending on the phase of her menstrual cycle, a woman may desire different "types" of partners, looking at characteristics such as suitability for long-term partnership or markers of virility. Similarly, testosterone level is known to have a large impact on sexual desire in men; low testosterone levels are generally associated with low interest in sexual activity overall. Other hormones, such as oxytocin, likely play a role in a man's libido as well, although these are not well described and currently have little relevance in clinical assessments. It is important to note that while "setting the stage" for sexual desire and overall interest, the hormonal milieu of any given person is not usually the defining factor in sexual behaviors.

The cognitive component of libido is also very important. Many people can summon an image of the ideal partner and setting for sexual activities. The richness of this visualization varies, of course, but might include the physical appearance of the person, perhaps the smell of a particular cologne or perfume, and the ambience of the setting, including temperature, location, and furnishings. These preferences are established and evolve over the life of the individual. The general outlines of these preferences usually become more established with age and experience. Sometimes, the origin of these preferred ideas and characteristics can be traced to specific events or experiences, and sometimes they cannot.

THE HUMAN SEXUAL RESPONSE CYCLE

The human body's response to erotic stimulation is one of the best examples of its complex function, demonstrating clearly that mind and body are not separate but are entirely integrated, albeit in ways that we imperfectly understand. The human sexual response cycle can be divided into four phases: desire, arousal, maintenance, and climax. Each of these phases depends on different aspects of the human anatomy and physiology.[4]

Desire

The desire that arises and flares up from time to time relies on critical inputs that come from the sensory organs, especially visual and smell but the other senses as well. Sensory inputs such as these are continually processed by the brain and checked against previous experiences to gauge the degree of sexual desire appropriate for the moment. Certain cues from the environment, such as a cold shower, can also dramatically suppress sexual desire.

Perhaps the most "cognitive," or brain cell–intensive, phase of the sexual response cycle, this does not mean that desire is necessarily consciously determined. Much of the processing of sensory stimuli is not apparent to the individual, and desire can appear without much apparent warning. The phase of desire is also profoundly affected by conscious thoughts, however, and desire can be manipulated through cognitive processes. For example, the sensory stimuli can be enhanced by thinking of fantasies or elaborations of the actual experience. On the other hand, the stimulation can be calmed down through the distractions of nonerotic and mundane, unrelated thoughts.

A conscious preference for a certain physical characteristic in a sexual partner can be learned and become a necessary factor to experience desire. Sometimes, a certain smell or taste could trigger an urge of desire. Similarly, negative preferences can also accumulate, so a different smell could result in an aversion to initiating or engaging in sexual behaviors. Conscious thoughts or cognitive activity (e.g., nervous ruminations) that distract the brain from processing inputs critical to sexual desire can interfere with the development and recognition of desire and short-circuit the sexual response as well as inhibit the longer-term retention of potential sensory preferences.

The actual neural circuitry involved in the processing of sensory inputs and checking the brain's historical notes on what is and is not desirable is not exactly known. The brain stem and thalamus are clearly critical to the processing of sensory inputs. The frontal lobe cortex is essential for maintaining a sense of what is and is not socially acceptable. The memory centers in the hippocampus are also involved, and the actual nerve cells connecting these hubs of activity project across the brain and involve serotonin and dopamine receptors for transmission. Although the details are not certain, many aspects of brain function are critical to sexual desire.

Arousal

Arousal is the translation of desire, the first phase of the sexual response, from the brain into the body. This is mediated through electrochemical impulses transmitted through nerves via the spinal cord, the autonomic nervous system, the network of motor nerves spread throughout the body, and hormones (chemicals that communicate between cells) transported through the blood.

Together, the nerves and hormones activated as a result of growing desire lead to arousal. This is detectable in women as engorgement of the vulva and clitoris and lubrication of the vagina and external genitalia. In men, it is most apparent as an erection, the equivalent engorgement of the penis, resulting in an increase in its length, girth, and stiffness. Systemic effects in both men and women include increased sweating, increased secretions of the apocrine sweat glands, flushing of the skin from dilation of the capillary beds, and quickened pulse and respiratory rate.

Maintenance

The ability to maintain the sexual response requires a balance of processes driving toward climax and pulling back toward baseline quiescence. The maintenance phase is a very intricate period in which all aspects of the process—the different sensory inputs from the genitals and the entire body, the emotional context, and the cognitive activities—interact and must sustain the right mix for continued sexual activity. If arousal is the translation of desire from the brain to the body, maintenance requires an equivalent communication of pleasurable sensory inputs from the body to the brain. If any domain is disturbed, the balance required in the maintenance phase is lost, and sexual arousal can reverse remarkably quickly ("kill the mood") or progress to the point of no return (orgasm or climax).

Climax (Orgasm and Ejaculation)

This phase of the sexual response represents the profound culmination of desire and arousal and marks the successful physiologic end of the maintenance phase. In the periphery, climax is marked by rhythmic contractions of muscles in the pelvic girdle and genitals and resultant pulsatile extrusion of secretions from the various glands in both men and women. Of course, climax in the man usually (but not always) coincides with ejaculation from the penis of semen, that is, all of the secretions from the prostate, seminal vesicles, and testicles carrying sperm.

In the brain, climax is notable for electrochemical inputs stimulating the reward centers of the brain, releasing dopamine and saturating the nerve cells responsible for perceiving pleasure. Orgasm is one of the most rewarding stimulatory events from the brain's perspective. It creates a sometimes overwhelming feeling of desire for more sexual activity.

Refractory Period

After climax, both men and women experience a period in which arousal is not possible. The components necessary for the involved nerves and hormones to take desire from the brain back out to the periphery are depleted and must be built up again before further sexual activity. This refractory period varies from person to person and even with each episode. The refractory period increases with age but also is affected by nutritional status, baseline hormone levels, and other factors.

The Sexual Response and Relationships

The powerful reward feelings generated by climax can serve to bond partners together into more durable relationships. The shared experience of losing one's head in the semireflexive sexual response and baring the most sensitive parts of the body to each other often results in a special set of feelings for the partner. These can confer a special, more intimate status to the relationship. These feelings solidify baseline interest in the partner and can reinforce other factors, such as societal expectations for married couples. The intense feelings experienced at climax are an independent physiologic output, however, and can become associated or confused with negative feelings and traumatic memories if experienced in the context of negative sexual activities, such as sexual trauma.

SUMMARY

Sexual health and function are important aspects of overall health. The sexual response is a powerful integration of complex central and peripheral body systems that is partly conscious and partly generated reflexively by the body. Ideally, the intense pleasure generated by climax serves to reinforce a special bond with one's partner.

2

MILITARY CONTEXT AND CULTURE

WHY WORRY ABOUT SEXUAL DYSFUNCTION IN A MILITARY POPULATION?

Sexual dysfunction is a common problem in the general U.S. population and is at least as common in military and veteran groups. Direct evidence shows that 20 to 30 percent of recent veterans of Iraq and Afghanistan seeking care through the Veterans Health Administration report sexual health issues. Similarly aged people (20 to 35 years old) from the general U.S. population report rates of sexual health issues closer to 10 to 15 percent. Among recent combat veterans presenting to a clinic at a Veterans Administration medical center for the first time, less than 10 percent had a sexual health issue documented in their medical record. Within six months, that rate had risen to 24 percent, or almost one in four veterans.[1]

There are several reasons why deployed veterans might experience more difficulty with sexual function and their sexual health might suffer. Several factors known to contribute to sexual dysfunction are more common among military personnel deployed to combat. For example, posttraumatic stress disorder (PTSD), depression, and anxiety are all problems that can develop after combat and are more common in military groups than in the general U.S. population. These can contribute directly to sexual dysfunction and impair sexual health. In addition, medications are often prescribed to treat these conditions, some of which may contribute to sexual dysfunction. Finally, sexual health is dependent on the social setting, and for many service members, their deployment significantly disrupts their relationships and support network to a great extent and compromises their sexual health. Many of these stressors are not as common in the general U.S. population, likely contributing to the higher rate of sexual dysfunction and lower sexual health among recently deployed veterans and service members.

Some of these factors can be perpetuated throughout the individual's life, and their impact on sexual health can contribute to lifelong challenges. PTSD, for example, is often a chronic condition with symptoms that wax and wane. Some Vietnam veterans still require medications to help manage these symptoms, and the adverse effects of the medications on sexual function may exacerbate limitations in sexual function due to other health problems that are related to aging. Preferences and behaviors ingrained while in the military or soon after separation may continue to color the psychosocial milieu of a former military person and his or her partners.

For these reasons, this book focuses on the sexual health of current and former military personnel, highlighting some of the distinctive factors that might influence their sexuality throughout their life.

HOW IS SEXUAL HEALTH AFFECTED BY THE MILITARY?

It is always risky to make generalizations about a group of people, especially if people do not necessarily see themselves as members of a "group." This is a particular challenge when talking about veterans and military service members; current and former military personnel are not really a single group of people. In fact, there are perhaps more differences and important distinctions within this group than there are similarities. The rivalries between different branches of the service (e.g., army versus navy) are legendary, and most military units have celebrated and distinctive traditions of heroism and historic contributions in their service to the United States. While recognizing the important diversity within this group that we call veterans and military service members, this book aims to deliver information of relevance and importance to people who share the experience of military service, especially service in a theater of conflict or war. This chapter explores some themes that justify the broad focus on current and former U.S. military personnel.

MILITARY CULTURE AND POLICY

War is a distinct activity best executed using certain practices and structures demonstrated over time to lead to success. Warriors and support personnel must learn the necessary skills to accomplish the tasks required of them for success. Some of the practices and structures necessary to succeed at war are not consistent with other settings, occupations, or relationships. This book is not intended as an indictment of military organizations or necessarily as a call for change. Rather, it points out some of the potential consequences of military service on the sexual health of those who serve in this vital calling.

For millennia, war has been fought and managed using top-down, hierarchical management processes and organizational structures. These features facilitate knowing one's role on the team and the specific responsibilities and duties required of that role. In the context of the life-threatening danger of combat and explicit dependence on other team members for mission success and survival, tightly controlled, coordinated organizations are critical. Training and operating in this type of organization creates a culture of accountability to one's immediate supervisor and loyalty to the team. There is explicit discouragement of questioning. You receive an order, and you carry it out. This approach has been very effective in most combat situations, hence the continued emphasis of modern militaries on chains of command and minute attention to organizational and operational details.[2]

To disseminate and enforce practices and standards deemed effective, the U.S. military, like armed forces around the world, develops policies to guide practice across the organization. In the United States, policies differ among the branches (i.e., army, navy, and air force) and components (i.e., active duty, National Guard, and reserves) but are generally coordinated across the Department of Defense. The Uniform Code of Military Justice (UCMJ) outlines the commonalities of the legal system of justice and includes several articles relevant to sexual health and behaviors. Unit commanders and their officers have a degree of leeway, however, in implementing policies and enforcing the rules at a local, or unit, level.[3] This results in a wide range of experiences for service members.

The policies of the Department of Defense contribute directly to the overall U.S. military "culture" and the shaping of individuals' attitudes, beliefs, and behaviors. Relative to the broader American culture, the policies of the military and their implementation have historically produced a male-dominated, heterosexually oriented culture with tightly defined "rules of engagement" for sexual activity. The extent of attention to the violation of these rules and the interpretation of the more subjective rules lead to some variation in execution. To the extent that the culture of the U.S. military differs in these domains from the broader U.S. civilian society and culture, current and former military personnel may react to news, events, and trends related to sexual health and behaviors in ways that are more similar to each other and differ significantly from the reactions of those who have not served in the military.

The most relevant examples for our discussion of sexual health are the policies that directly govern sexual activity among service members. The term "fraternization" refers to inappropriate interactions between service members, including sexual activity, that undermine unit and command structure and cohesion. Army Regulation 600-20, paragraph 4-14, for example, specifies which relationships between enlisted personnel and officers are allowed. The rules specifically highlight sexual relations or even the appearance of intimacy. Rules about fraternization aim to minimize conflicts between individuals that might arise from sexual activity or other behaviors and disrupt unit morale and performance. Consequences of violating these rules can include counseling, training, demotion, or even courts-martial (military criminal proceedings).[4] Given that most active duty military personnel are 18 to 25 years old and male and thus at the peak of their sexual activity, constructing and enforcing rules for sexual activity is a time-proven necessity.

Similarly, the concept of "conduct unbecoming" is a catchall construct that provides a backstop for maintaining the necessary order in the organization. Vaguely defined, the subjective nature of "conduct unbecoming" is applied by commanding officers to subordinates caught engaging in problematic behaviors, often including those of a sexual nature.[5] Part of the UCMJ, these rules about association among service members and unacceptable behaviors implicitly recognize the centrality of sexual health and behaviors to human nature but attempt to set parameters for appropriate manifestation of these human needs and desires in the military setting.

Another visible example of policy relevant to sexual health is the set of rules governing the role of women in the military. Women played a very small formal role in U.S. military activities until after World War II. Historically, the policies of the U.S. military have restricted the involvement of women to specific roles and locations, and only very recently (2013) have women been formally allowed to serve in actual combat roles.[6] These policies, plus other, broader societal factors, have limited women's interest and ability to join the military. The number of women in the military, although increasing, remains low (about 12 percent women across the services). This is in stark contrast to the participation of women in the civilian workforce across the entire range of jobs. The paucity of women in the military creates a very male-dominated culture that colors many aspects of military life.

A third example of relevance to sexual health is the U.S. military policy toward homosexuality in military service members. Most obviously affecting people who identify as gay, lesbian, or bisexual (GLB), these rules have a broader impact on military culture as well. Once again, recent changes in policy highlight the tension between evolving societal norms and their impact on military culture and vice versa. Long-standing rules were likely first implemented to reduce the opportunity for discord among U.S. troops related to same-sex sexual activity. This focus reflects the especially marginalized status of homosexuality in the United States historically.

A major shift occurred after passage of the "don't ask, don't tell" law in the 1990s. This law shifted the focus from criminal prosecution of homosexual activities by active duty service members to personnel actions, including discharge from service. This shift reduced the burden of substantiating claims for full prosecution, but made it easier to expel GLB service members. In fact, the number of GLB service members discharged from the military for being homosexual, although not necessarily engaging in homosexual activity, actually increased. Many received regular discharges, although some were discharged with less-than-honorable designations.[7] The threat of having one's sexuality discovered and resulting in the termination of one's military career compelled many GLB service members to suppress and hide their sexuality and compromise their sexual health to continue to serve.

Until recently, sodomy, or "unnatural carnal copulation," understood as oral and anal sexual activity and often considered the primary forms of sexual activity by same-sex partners, was forbidden among active duty military personnel. By 2013, as GLB issues became more openly discussed in U.S. society generally, they also surfaced in the military culture, and the article addressing sodomy in the UCMJ was amended to limit the prosecution of sodomy to cases of forced or nonconsensual acts only.

The recent regulatory and policy changes related to GLB service members and their activities have shifted the official military structure and processes closer to the broader U.S. cultural mainstream. This shift was prompted perhaps in part by the loss of highly trained and effective military personnel and recognition of the growing discrepancy between military policy and growing acceptance of GLB people in mainstream America.[8] In fact, by recognizing same-sex marriages in 2013 and extending employment benefits to same-sex partners, the Department of Defense has gone further than most states in promoting equal rights for same-sex couples. As of mid-2014, transgender individuals are still prohibited from serving in the military. Service members who realize and take steps to implement gender reassignment are in violation of military policy and will be discharged. These changes are still reverberating around the organization, and reactions at the unit level will likely vary.

MARRIAGE

In earlier eras, the UCMJ spoke explicitly about male service members and treated a civilian woman married to a male service member as an extension of him, in accordance with other legal traditions. The implied message was that, once married, women became extensions of the male service member and lost the right to speak or act independently. This changed by the 1970s, but many living veterans completed their military service in this context.

MILITARY CULTURAL INFLUENCES ON SEXUAL HEALTH

The official policies and rules governing some key factors directly and indirectly related to sexual health contribute substantially to military culture. They also exert both subtle and overt effects on the sexual health and behaviors of current and former U.S. military personnel. Individuals who serve in the military must adapt to the prevailing organizational culture to succeed. For some, this might require significant changes or accommodations to their premilitary and still evolving sexual attitudes, beliefs, and behaviors. For others, the culture may reinforce these characteristics and, in fact, might have been an important consideration in their decision to join the military in the first place. Either way, when military service is done, the individual must return to a civilian society and culture that might differ significantly from what he or she knew in service.

In any hierarchical organization, the structure and processes can become too rigid, and perspectives can become narrow and self-serving. This can result in significant barriers to change and inflexibility to adapt to new environments or externalities. When policies become outdated relative to broader societal norms or the standards of similar, peer organizations, or competitors, the divergence can result in conflict, impaired performance, or both. Individuals may be challenged by competing loyalties or demoralized and confused. Recent shifts in the military policies toward the roles of women service members, GLB service members, and sexual trauma likely reflect organizational adjustments to improve alignment with broader U.S. culture and its evolving ideas about sexual health.

SEX-BASED ROLES AND EXPECTATIONS

Given the long-standing institutionalized differences in roles for service men and women, there is no question about sex being a prominent differentiating factor in military culture. There are also several highly publicized phenomena that likely relate to the sex-based differences in roles and expectations. First, the number of women leaders in the military hierarchy is low relative to many private sector industries. Second, women service members continue to serve primarily in certain occupations and jobs (intelligence, community relations, and health care) and not in others (infantry). The integration of women into military service is only partial and has contributed to a perception of women service members as second-class citizens.

These facets of military life may be perceived by some to reinforce two stereotypes that may influence sexual health and behavior. The first stereotype is the belief that women are subservient or submissive and not able to succeed in the military. Although there may not be a direct line of evidence, the rarity of encountering a woman in a position of authority at work in the military likely perpetuates a belief (in some) that women not only don't have authority in the current reality but also *shouldn't* be in charge. Second, by reinforcing sex-based differentiation of training and responsibilities and deemphasizing the true skills, knowledge, and aptitude of the individual, the stereotypical differences between men and women are emphasized. Once again, some may extrapolate from the imperfect but visible reality to presume that all women and men belong in certain roles and positions rather than acknowledging the primacy of individual strengths and weaknesses relative to differences between men and women. Perpetuating the belief that "all women are ——— and all men are ———" misses the point that, in some instances, large proportions of men and women are more similar than all women are to each other. In the context of sexual health and behaviors, these prejudices can result in misjudgments about sexual orientation and preferences and intolerance for the normal variations within each sex.

RISKY SEXUAL BEHAVIOR

Another observation possibly linked to military policies and cultural influences is increased risk taking among current and former service members. Reliable figures are difficult to obtain, but anecdotally and based on published rates of sexually transmitted disease treatment, military personnel tend to engage in sexual activity with more partners and with lower rates of barrier protection than peers who are not in the military.[9] Confining sexual activity to off-base locations during the relatively limited off-duty time and primarily with nonmilitary personnel leaves a limited realm of possibilities for engaging in sexual activity.

Relative to their civilian peers, young service members may experience severely constrained opportunities to engage in sexual activity with non-military personnel. This may contribute to risky choices, including employing sex workers, engaging in anonymous or casual sex, or having unprepared and therefore unprotected sex.

The fatalism experienced by some service members before a deployment may foster the attitude that a warrior should seize the day because he or she might not live to see another. This can lead to decisions about sexual activity and relationships that may not be consistent with sexual health or broader long-term health.

While binge drinking is common among young people (18 to 25 years old) across U.S. society, it may be more problematic among military personnel in this age range. For example, well-intentioned rules to ban alcohol consumption on a military base may contribute to binge drinking off base at parties, bars, and other settings. Binge drinking is known to be associated with risky sexual behavior through impaired judgment. Marginalizing alcohol use by relegating it to social activities that are poorly integrated with official military life and positive influences can be problematic. This can have the unintended consequence of increasing the chances of bad decisions about sexual activities and higher rates of risky or inappropriate sexual behavior. Limiting access to alcohol on base may reduce the risk of on-base alcohol-related complications but may contribute to concentrated overindulgence and poor judgments in unmonitored settings.

Finally, a heterosexual, male-dominated culture may also promote risky sexual behavior through peer pressure. In an age-group still defining their sexuality, young men in particular may test boundaries and experiment in ways that increase their risk of sexually transmitted diseases, unwanted pregnancy, or even legal problems. In an attempt to obtain feedback and elicit peer approval, they may share these exploits and live vicariously through the actions of each other, often pushing to test the limits of acceptability. Women service members similarly experience peer pressure, although it may be expressed and experienced differently, which can drive behaviors that may diminish sexual health. Once established, unhealthy peer pressure can be difficult to eradicate from an organization. Also, for the individual, risky sexual behavior may become the pattern of behavior—part of his or her sexuality—even when the reinforcing factors are no longer operating.

SEXUAL TRAUMA

One of the tragic aspects of human sexual behavior, sexual trauma is a reality for many military personnel, both male and female. Once again, the policies sketched above may contribute to the occurrence of sexual trauma in a military setting, albeit unintentionally. Women's contributions to military success, especially when the warrior or killer role has been officially forbidden to them, might be minimized by some. It may be perceived that because of the limited stereotyped sex-based roles and responsibilities for women in the military, they are second-class citizens. This subtle devaluation of women service members might contribute to a perceived justifiability for sexual harassment or even for imposing sexual activity on women. The value on masculinity in military culture may similarly be exaggerated and misconstrued to tolerate aggression and dominance, especially toward men and women perceived as weak or vulnerable. These are not conscious, linear thought processes but rather background that can color attitudes, beliefs, and perhaps behavior. The prevalence of sexual trauma and harassment reported and suspected but unreported in the military suggests a pervasive if unspoken cultural complacency toward its presence.

The UCMJ is very clear about the prosecution and punishment of many aspects of sexual violence, outlining specific types of activities and applicable processes for handling transgressions. There has been continued and increasing concern about the effectiveness or even the unintended consequences of these rules. While military leaders, grassroots-level advocates, and government overseers grapple with this situation, its impact on the sexual health and function of current and former service members will likely remain palpable.

The effects of sexual trauma are often most direct and dramatic on the women and men who suffer through the trauma themselves but also impact the sexual health of the perpetrators, conspirators, witnesses, and even those who know something happened but weren't present. When severe or experienced repetitively or chronically, sexual trauma can have major impacts on overall health, mental and emotional health, and sexual health and the interest and ability to engage in sexual activity.

SEPARATION FROM INTIMATE PARTNERS AND FAMILY

When thinking about military service and deployment in particular, the theme of separation comes to the fore. Training for and deploying to a foreign conflict has often been a 12- to 18-month obligation since 2001. This separates the service members from their established social supports and activities and puts them at significant risk of their degradation or permanent disruption. Recent combat deployments have relied heavily on the National Guard and reserve components of the military. These service men and women tend to be older with more established families and partners as well as jobs and other obligations in civilian society. Many in the active duty component are likewise partnered and have established socialization patterns and intimate relationships that are similarly disrupted by deployment.

Given the central role of sexual health and activity to the overall well-being of humans and their relationships, these separations can be fraught with new challenges for couples. Each member of the couple may experience significant changes in roles and responsibilities, perhaps only out of necessity at first but then sometimes with previously unrealized interest. Profound psychological and metaphysical changes during combat can alter the personality and beliefs of the service member. Self-discoveries and new awareness can also occur in the stateside partner. This can make the reunion between the two difficult and create a challenging period of reintroduction requiring a great deal of attention and nurturing.

SUMMARY

These themes and resultant phenomena underscore the premise that military veterans and service members are similarly exposed to cultural influences through their military service and combat deployments that may impact their sexual health and function. Despite the pervasive nature of these influences, they do not destine the individual to a particular sexual health status or set of behaviors or problems. In fact, the characteristics of each individual are far more important to his or her own particular circumstances. This is especially important to remember when addressing a challenge in one's own or a partner's sexual health and function. Understanding the military culture and its sequelae may facilitate understanding and acceptance within the relationship.

3

EFFECTS OF COMBAT DEPLOYMENT ON HEALTH

Those returning from combat experience health problems far different from those experienced by the general population. These include chronic pain from musculoskeletal injuries, traumatic brain injury (TBI), posttraumatic stress disorder (PTSD) and other mental health conditions, sleep disruption, and social disruption. Recent, large combat deployments including Operations Iraqi Freedom and Enduring Freedom (TBI), the first Gulf War (Gulf War illness), and Vietnam (Agent Orange exposure) have resulted in specific, or signature, effects that affect the health of anyone who served during those military engagements.

In chapter 2, we discussed some of the military policies and related military cultural factors that might impact the sexual health and function of any person who served in the military. Beyond the policies and the dominant culture, there are some near universal experiences, such as boot camp, physical training and fitness testing, living in barracks, standing in long lines, communal eating in the chow hall, and shopping in military commissaries, just to name a few.

Combat, on the other hand, is not experienced by everyone in the military. There are many military personnel stateside supporting those who deploy to the combat theater. Once again, it is critical to point out that the deployment experience is unique for every individual despite being at the exact same base at the same time. In this chapter, we discuss the more concrete consequences of war and combat.

VISIBLE WOUNDS OF WAR

War is a noisy, dirty, dangerous activity, and participating in war can have dramatic effects on an individual's health and function. There are the obvious aftereffects of war: death and injury from enemy bullets, explosions, friendly fire, and combat activity–related accidents. The individual's chance of experiencing these varies depending on job or occupation, actual assigned duties, and where one is based.

The proportion of combatants experiencing these complications of war varies by conflict given different combat environments, weapons being used, and intensity of fighting. A striking trend in the course of military history is the decrease in the proportion of troops killed in action and in theater in every U.S. conflict since the Civil War. Because of new protective measures and advances in medical care, more of the seriously injured are surviving, and the proportion of troops who return home with serious structural damage to their body and persistent dysfunction has increased.

Forward-based medical expertise and lifesaving technologies have improved survival for the seriously injured. The absolute number of veterans who served in Iraq and Afghanistan living with "polytrauma," that is, significant damage to more than one body system or functional unit, is approximately 10,000 (out of more than 2.6 million U.S. troops deployed).[1] This includes veterans with limb amputations, serious head injury, and serious injuries to other internal organs and body systems.

The resultant injuries to the body structure are sometimes permanent or never return to baseline, and many are readily apparent. For example, when you're missing an arm, it's usually pretty obvious to others. A structural defect like that doesn't just go away. These injuries are usually quickly recognized and addressed with surgery, rehabilitation, prostheses, or other interventions by the military health care system, Veterans Health Administration, or civilian health care delivery systems. These injuries are also more quickly and easily recognized in terms of honors and other formal indications of appreciation. For example, the Purple Heart is awarded to service members with physical injuries in the course of battle.[2] Finally, military personnel with injuries impacting body structure are often compensated monetarily through military group life insurance policies, military medical and pension retirement benefits with loss of fitness for duty, or through Veterans Benefits Administration service-connection benefits.

The downstream effects of these visible injuries can be huge for the individual, his or her family, and society as a whole. Consider, for example, veterans who are severely disabled from serious TBIs and other injuries sustained in improvised explosive device blasts and other attacks. These individuals are usually young (less than 30 years old), can become completely dependent on others for daily activities necessary for life, and are no longer able to fully participate in society as they or their families had originally planned. Because they are young and thanks to advances in medical care, many of these seriously injured veterans will live to old age with high levels of need for personal and health care as well as attendance to the emotional and mental effects of such injuries.[3]

David survived a catastrophic brain injury. His wife, Susan, was not sure if David was even aware of her or their daughter's presence, although she wanted to believe this. David was minimally responsive to any stimuli and was completely dependent on his wife and the paid caregivers supporting the family 24 hours a day at home.

Ted was a double amputee, missing his left arm below the elbow and the left leg from just above the knee. His leg had become infected, and he and the salvage team, after many operations, decided to allow the stump to heal even though he was likely to have recurrent infections in the upper leg bone. Luckily, Ted found a job as a consultant for a large company and was doing quite well. About once a year, he would develop a low-grade fever and not feel so well and then start a course of antibiotics to suppress the osteomyelitis (bone infection) in his leg. In the three years since separating from the army, Ted also had recurrent episodes of blood in his semen, usually around the time of the osteomyelitis flare-up. He couldn't see any damage to his genitals but wondered whether there was damage inside his testicles.

Doris, the mother of another veteran with a severe head injury, Edward, wondered whether her never-married son, in his early twenties, would ever find a girlfriend or wife and enjoy an intimate, loving relationship. Edward was mobile and able to engage in social activities but required a walker and supervision when out of the house. He sometimes chafed at his lack of independence but in general recognized his limitations and made the best of his situation.

Clarissa was a woman veteran in her mid-thirties who experienced a back injury while deployed and then complications of a back surgery to fix the problem. She was confined to a motorized wheelchair outside of the house due to weakness and pain in her legs and also experienced urinary incontinence. She had to move in with her parents to ensure the safety and optimize the living conditions for her daughter and herself. She was never married, and now that she had to respect her parents' wishes to not have visitors in the house, she perceived that her dating days were over. She also had to cope with the reality that she may never have more children of her own.

Juan experienced a severe head injury, and his wife left him with their children and severely limited his contact with them. Sad and angry about his wife leaving him, his mother had Juan move back to the city where she lived so she could assist him. Juan lived in a group home due to self-control issues from his brain injury and resented the loss of autonomy and privacy. He wasn't usually physically aggressive, but he would get loud and insistent, and he was a big guy, weighing almost 300 pounds. In addition, his pituitary gland wasn't working properly, requiring him to take various hormone supplements and contributing to his obesity, prediabetes, and sexual dysfunction.

A common thread in these examples is the veterans' persistent dependence on others as well as assistive equipment or environmental adaptations. This decrease in autonomy can have a profound impact on all aspects of life, including sexuality and sexual function. Also, each of these veterans experienced varying degrees of limitations in function that may preclude certain activities even with accommodations. Their dependence will require assistance for many decades to come. Fortunately, there is a great deal of support available to these heroes who have sacrificed so much and carry the visible evidence of their dedication.

INVISIBLE WOUNDS OF WAR

While the visible wounds might generate the most attention, there are even more combat veterans who carry the invisible scars of war. For some of these individuals, the challenges created by the damage also impede their daily function. The source of their challenges, however, is not apparent to others. They have the additional burden of proving to others that they are broken. These invisible wounds include chronic pain, PTSD, mild TBI, sleep disruptions, and others.

Pain

Moderate damage to bodily structure, as opposed to the serious damage described above, is even more prevalent and can still result in chronic effects, especially pain and dysfunction. Trauma and overuse injuries of the musculoskeletal system are common in military training, operations, and deployment. These injuries are not unexpected, and, despite attempts to prevent them, inevitably they occur. Even with appropriate interventions, including rest, physical rehabilitation, and surgery, recovery and healing can be very long and often incomplete, leaving the individual with residual dysfunction and pain. Statistics from the Veterans Health Administration Office of Public Health indicate that musculoskeletal diagnoses are among the most common recorded for veterans using the Veterans Health Administration, being present in more than 60 percent of veterans of Iraq and Afghanistan. Service connection for disability related to musculoskeletal injuries experienced during or exacerbated by military service represents a large proportion of all granted claims.[4]

Common musculoskeletal problems, such as chronic low back, hip, and knee pain, are not unique to current and former military personnel, and information from the general U.S. population is helpful. Much of what we know about chronic musculoskeletal pain and how it impacts a person's life is not specific to veterans and service members. These are among the most common diagnoses recorded in health care encounters in the United States in general and are associated with many days of lost productivity and huge health care expenses. Anyone who has experienced low back pain (which is one in two Americans per year) can understand how this can affect daily functioning, whether at work, at home, or in bed.

Jack did more than 100 patrols on foot "outside the wire" while deployed to Iraq. He routinely carried more than 80 pounds of equipment and his machine gun while hiking over rough terrain and having to occasionally chase suspects through villages and towns. He had numerous falls and was often sore and bruised. He had a couple of more serious falls, and by the end of the deployment, he realized his right leg was going numb. While out-processing, his military medical team gave him ibuprofen, an anti-inflammatory, and when that didn't seem to work, they tried hydrocodone, an opioid pain reliever that can also be addicting. Eventually, he and his provider team realized that he had a pinched nerve, and they decided to try back surgery to fix it.

Of course, sometimes it's harder to see the musculoskeletal injuries and the pain and dysfunction they cause. The impact of chronic pain on behaviors can be difficult to pin down. Friends, family, coworkers, and even acquaintances may wonder if the pain is really bad enough to disrupt participation or if there is something else going on. Only the person suffering the pain really knows, although almost always there are multiple contributing factors. These factors include the pain itself and the dysfunction of the limb or joint associated with the pain but also the emotions, fears, and thoughts surrounding the pain experience. For reasons like these, some musculoskeletal injuries and the resultant pain can become a point of contention in a relationship, especially when the pain is interfering with participation in social events, including sexual activity.

TBI

TBI is the disruption of function as the result of an external force to the brain. It is classified as mild, moderate, or severe by the American College of Rehabilitative Medicine. TBI is often accompanied by other, outwardly visible signs of injury as described in the examples above, but sometimes it causes disruption to normal brain or bodily function in isolation, or these issues may remain after the visible problems have healed.

Experts estimate that up to 300,000 troops who served in Iraq and Afghanistan may have experienced one or more TBI. Most TBIs in military service members, whether from direct impact or related to blast exposures, are mild. Mild TBI, or concussions, are traditionally thought of as temporary, or self-limited, conditions with full recovery happening in most people within three months of injury. This is the case with deployment-related mild TBI as well; most military service members recover completely and have no lasting effects from mild TBI.

There is growing evidence, however, that even mild TBI can result in longer-lasting problems, at least in a subset of those injured. Symptoms that are sometimes attributed to mild TBI include cognitive difficulties, such as attention, memory, and decision-making problems. These can interfere with everyday activities in a profound but often subtle way. Headaches can persist or recur after TBI. They range from dull aches that persist over extended periods or may be more intense and migraine-like. Photosensitivity can be problematic for some, and tinnitus, or ringing in the ears, is a common annoyance. Often, friends and family note that the injured veteran has a different personality.

The impact of these injuries varies remarkably, and there is currently no definitive way to determine the importance of mild TBI in an individual relative to other problems that are often present as well. In many individuals, mild TBI is accompanied by PTSD, chronic pain from musculoskeletal damage, depression, or sleep disruption. Trying to figure out which symptom goes with which problem is often impossible and perhaps unimportant. A veteran with a troublesome combination of these problems needs a comprehensive, systematic evaluation and management plan and ongoing attention.[5]

Detecting abnormalities in the brain structures related to mild TBI is very challenging. Current clinical methods, such as magnetic resonance imaging (MRI), have the resolution power to detect only gross abnormalities in brain structure, the ones that would be visible to the naked eye. It is thought that some of the critical damage in mild TBI may be at the level of the brain cells and layers and microscopic connections between certain areas. Newer MRI methods that are not part of standard clinical practice yet—such as functional MRI, which looks at actual brain cell function in specific areas of the brain, not just structural integrity, and diffusion tensor imaging (DTI), which looks at the connections between different parts of the brain—also do not have adequate resolution to pinpoint the damage.

Joe had a moderate TBI; he was unconscious for about 45 minutes, had amnesia of the event and a few hours before it, and took several days to recover from the headaches, dizziness, and memory problems. When he had an MRI of his brain about three years after the event, it was read by the radiologist as "normal." This seemed almost impossible to Joe's wife, Megan, at the time, given Joe's continued difficulties with memory and concentration. In addition, Joe's primary care doctor had told them that his decreased interest in sex and difficulty with arousal might be related to his head injury. Megan grilled Joe's doctors about the possibility of other tests that could be done.

Joe was told that he was eligible for a research protocol that used functional MRI and DTI to study the effects of TBI on memory. Outside of that protocol, his doctors, including the neurologist and rehabilitation medicine specialist, assured him that there were no other tests that would provide more detailed information about the actual damage to the brain. Joe went ahead with the research study, figuring that others might benefit from his participation but did not receive copies or interpretations of the functional MRI or DTI images, as they were considered for research only. Joe and Megan had to accept the limitations in their knowledge of the exact nature of his brain damage. Joe was happy to be able to participate in the study in the hopes that someday he, or another veteran like him, might benefit from its finding.

With the large investment in TBI research, it is likely that we will continue to learn more about which people are more likely to develop persistent problems from TBI and what we can do to help them. The current standard of care for veterans with TBI focuses on supporting the symptomatic veteran by identifying compensatory strategies using a biopsychosocial approach and optimizing the management of the other health conditions that are also present.

PTSD

PTSD is the persistent reaction to a perceived life-threatening traumatic experience that manifests as hyperarousal, isolation, reexperiencing, and hypervigilance and that interferes with the successful accomplishment of everyday activities for the individual. PTSD manifests differently in different people. The various symptoms wax and wane, and the effects of PTSD may vary, depending on which symptoms are most prominent and problematic at the time.

PTSD is common after trauma, including combat, affecting about 10 to 20 percent of combatants in any war.[6] In fact, many of the features of PTSD can actually be adaptive in the combat setting and become part of a disorder only when the individual can't adapt back to the civilian or nondeployment setting.

Hyperarousal can be described as a short temper, irritability, or a tendency to escalate problems or catastrophize challenges, especially those that are consciously or subconsciously associated with the original trauma (triggers). It is associated with increased activity of the body systems in the form of elevated heart rate and breathing as well as hormonal changes. Isolation is the tendency to avoid social contact, to withdraw from even well-intentioned supportive interactions. Reexperiencing trauma most commonly occurs as nightmares, very real dreams replaying the content of the trauma experience. Reexperiencing can also take the form of flashbacks, vivid daydreams that happen while awake and that interfere with functioning. The most severe forms of flashbacks can appear so real to the veteran that he or she believes they are actually occurring, like a hallucination. Finally, hypervigilance refers to the behaviors that reflect the individual's sense of vulnerability, such as double-checking locks, patrolling the home, stockpiling weapons, suspecting the motives of others, and trying to control situations and others' behavior.

Although PTSD is often perceived as a "psychological" disease by many, the symptoms of PTSD are actually the result of abnormalities in brain function. There are several theories that try to explain how these symptoms are caused and which parts of the brain are not working properly. One explanatory theme stresses an exaggerated fear response, the flight-or-fight response to a threat. A trigger that consciously or subconsciously reminds an individual of his or her trauma can push into a reflexive response to either fight one's way out of the situation or run away.

Julio's unit was attacked while on patrol in a busy market in Iraq. Julio's buddy was injured, and several locals, including a young girl, were killed, and there was blood everywhere. He wasn't able to get to his injured buddy right away and thought he was dead when he found him. Afterward, he had to help move the bodies into an ambulance. Since then, he's been reluctant to go out to crowded events and drinks beforehand to make it easier. If he doesn't, he feels his heart race, gets sweaty, and looks around everywhere for danger. Sometimes, he can't take it, and he just goes home. Occasionally, he'll try to stick it out but will end up in a fight.

Another underlying mechanism for PTSD symptoms may include dysfunctional learning by the brain. The premise of this theory is that there is inappropriate generalization of behaviors or reactions to stimuli that were learned in the context of a traumatic experience. Many veterans will identify with the scenario of a loud, unexpected noise, like a car backfiring in the parking lot of the local mall, causing them to drop instantly to the ground. Their brain has learned a new reflex response to a noise that it perceives as a gunshot.

Julio also drove on convoys while deployed. Several times, vehicles in his convoy were blown off the road by improvised explosive devices. He was never blown up while driving but was very careful to continuously look for unusual packages, trash, or signs of damage to the roads and to swerve around them. He also varied his speed but always went as fast as possible to minimize the risk of being hit by a rocket-propelled grenade. His friends won't ride with him now because he is "too aggressive" on the roads.

Both of these explanatory ideas invoke the presence of abnormal "circuits" in the brain. The circuits exist in everyone's brain, but because of particular, especially traumatic experiences and perhaps because of genetic predisposition, certain circuits are strengthened or weakened, and the brain function changes. These changes produce the behaviors and symptoms that we call PTSD. [7]

It is important to note that there are physiological markers of these changes in brain circuitry—it is not just the report of the individual or the observations by others of his or her behavior. These measures reflect the body's autonomic nervous system function, which is the circuitry that controls many of the basic, unconscious operating systems of the body, including blood vessel diameter and blood pressure, temperature, heart rate, and gastrointestinal function. Although imprecisely correlated and understood, individuals with PTSD have changes in brain waves during sleep, higher blood pressure (on average), different heart rate responses, different hormone levels, and other measurable differences when compared to similar individuals without PTSD.

Maria was deployed to Iraq in a combat support unit. She had a female battle buddy named Tamika, but when Tamika was sent home to help her dying mother, Maria found herself isolated among the rest of her unit. Her sergeant was increasingly aggressive and demeaning to her about her performance in the supply unit, shifting her to less desirable duties and shifts. One night, she found herself working alone when the sergeant appeared and forced her to perform fellatio on him, or he was going to "make her disappear." She was deathly afraid of him and complied and told no one. He would continue to show up at odd hours and repeat the demands for sexual activities. She never knew when this would happen and was terrified and felt disgusted with him, the military, and herself. When Maria returned home, she still couldn't tell anyone, especially her boyfriend, who didn't understand why Maria wasn't willing to reengage him in their intimate relationship. She even avoided social media connections with her unit because the sergeant was also active on the site.

Julio had different challenges when he returned to the states. His particular combat traumas were thousands of miles away, but the memories and effects of the trauma on his brain and body still affected his ability to interact socially. He had relocated to a new city looking for better employment opportunities and maybe to find a wife and settle down. Trying to get to know people, he went to a veterans' meet-up at a bar and ended up fighting with some civilian guys discussing the politics of a "war they never fought." He landed in jail for a night but was released without charges. He got a job as a security guard but was let go after numerous complaints about "his attitude" and "aggressive" behavior toward enforcing the rules. He collected unemployment and disability for his PTSD and damaged knee and decided it wasn't worth trying to find another job. He stopped trying to meet new people and hung out at home, not going to sleep until he checked all the doors and windows three times and put his loaded pistol under his pillow. He felt increasingly disconnected and held little hope for a good job or relationship.

PTSD is a chronic condition, and its symptoms can get worse and get better. There are also treatments that can improve the condition and help the individual manage the symptoms. Of course, as with any chronic condition, having a positive social support system can make it easier to thrive despite the illness. With optimal management, it is likely that the negative impact of PTSD on health can be reduced in most people. Unfortunately, many do not seek proper help or find it too challenging to continue to engage in treatment, and their uncontrolled PTSD symptoms continue to have a dramatic negative impact on their health and function.

Depression

Depression, a persistent state of low mood, hopelessness, lack of desire, low self-esteem, and low motivation, is a relatively common problem after deployment. Once again, although we define depression by the symptoms and self-reported perceptions and observed behavior and actions, it has its basis in brain and body system dysfunction. Often experienced by service members or veterans in conjunction with PTSD or physical injuries, depression may sometimes be difficult to recognize as an independent problem. It may seem that the person wouldn't be depressed if the other health problems weren't so bad.[8] It usually doesn't matter which came first; depression can and should be addressed simultaneously with other health problems.

Eventually, Maria and her boyfriend broke up. She withdrew more and more from friends and family, just not showing up for family events or celebrations. Although she was awake by 4:00 every morning, she sometimes wouldn't get out of bed until midday. She no longer did her hair or put on makeup. She started wondering if life was worth living.

Julio felt so bad about some of his experiences in public that he just stayed at home most of the time. He thought there was no chance he'd get a job, so he stopped applying. He began to feel worthless and hopeless. All the excitement he felt about moving to a new city to rebuild his life now vanished.

Feeling like hurting or killing oneself is a complication of depression and can be a terrifying experience. Although infrequently carried out, having suicidal thoughts like this suggests a very serious problem with depression and the urgent need for expert medical advice.

Substance Abuse

Unfortunately, alcohol and illicit substance abuse are also common problems for U.S. service members after deployment.[9] Of course, use of these substances is strictly regulated by law—alcohol can be consumed only within limits (below intoxication), in certain places (at home or in a licensed venue), and when certain activities (driving) are not happening. Similarly, legally available opioid pain medications, such as hydrocodone, morphine, and oxycodone, are disbursed only by a physician's prescription, and other opioids, such as heroin, are illegal.

Some people may have problems with substance use because they are trying to "self-medicate" their other problems, such as chronic pain or symptoms of PTSD. Too much alcohol or overuse of prescription medicines is almost always not the best solution, often leading to complications with health, health care, relationships, and the law.

Alcohol is a depressant, and although it can be somewhat effective at initiating sleep, masking pain, or suppressing PTSD symptoms, it has too many negative impacts on brain function and other body structures, such as the liver, to be considered helpful overall. Alcohol also clouds judgment and can contribute to making poor decisions.

Julio often drank a six-pack of beer at night before going to bed because it numbed the pain and made him forget his combat memories for a while. He still didn't feel rested in the morning and often had a dry mouth and a headache when he woke up. Within a couple of months of doing this, six beers didn't put him to sleep, and he was drinking 8 to 10 beers a night.

Jack took his hydrocodone pills for his back pain as prescribed but occasionally doubled up or took them with alcohol to try to get more relief when the pain was out of control. He would sometimes run out of pills before he was due for a refill and borrow some from a friend or try to get some more from the urgent care clinic.

Stimulants such as cocaine and methamphetamine are chemicals that accelerate thought processes and other body functions. Abuse of these can also be a problem after deployment. Stimulants can be attractive to some veterans because they generate many of the same physiologic responses experienced by some as the rush of combat during deployment. The body's reaction to these drugs can feel exciting and stimulate powerful reward circuits in the brain, making the individual want to do it again and again. The drugs themselves can cause damage to the brain and other body systems. Use of stimulants can cause addiction and result in unacceptable behaviors and damage to health and relationships.

Alcohol, opioids, stimulants, and other substances are best avoided when there is the possibility of an invisible wound of war. They are hard to use within healthy limits, and in the context of other deployment-related health issues, they generally do not promote overall health. The risks of their use usually outweigh any benefits.

Sleep Disruption

The general category of sleep disruption also registers as one of the more common and important postdeployment health issues. Sleep disruption is often multifactorial with many different factors contributing to the overall problem.[10] This complexity can make it challenging to know how to make it better. A systematic assessment and step-by-step action plan can be essential.

Postdeployment sleep problems can start during deployment. The opportunity to sleep during deployment can be a very rare occurrence, and good-quality sleep is an exception to the rule. Often, essential duties keep troops on the job for extended periods or with only brief opportunities to rest and recuperate. In addition, sleeping quarters and conditions are often suboptimal—noisy, smelly, crowded, and not secure. The largest deployments in the past 50 years have occurred to far parts of the globe, introducing significant time zone differences at the transitions between combat theater and home. The adjustments required for the time changes coming and going from theater and up-tempo operations can create a baseline challenge to sleep quality that escalates and spins out of control as other problems accrue.

Also, consider the sleep disruption caused by pain that may prevent or interrupt sleep. Sometimes, damage to musculoskeletal structures can make it difficult to find a comfortable sleeping position. For some, movements in the middle of the night can trigger pain and awaken the individual. With almost two-thirds of recent combat veterans experiencing chronic musculoskeletal pains, this is a very common sleep disruptor.

Jack could fall asleep if he positioned himself just right in his bed, but he often awoke in the middle of the night because of intense, sharp back pain. He would often take an extra pain pill before bed, and sometimes it seemed to help.

Mental health conditions can have a dramatic impact on sleep. For example, the hypervigilance associated with PTSD may make it hard for an individual to fall asleep, fearing for his or her safety. Separately, nightmares associated with PTSD disrupt sleep whether the individual awakens fully or not.

Tom always felt tired, especially when he was having his nightmares about combat. Every year around the time of his most intense fighting in the Battle of Fallujah, Tom would experience regular nightmares. He usually wouldn't remember waking up in the middle of the night but never felt refreshed in the morning.

Depression contributes to insomnia, making it difficult to fall asleep and causing the individual to wake up early, unrested but unable to fall back asleep. This is called terminal insomnia, the inability to sleep at the end of the night. It is a signature symptom of depression.

Maria found herself waking up every morning at 4:00 a.m. whether she set her alarm or not. She had no appointments that required her to get up that early, but she couldn't go back asleep despite still feeling low in energy. She would just stay in bed even though she couldn't sleep.

Substance abuse can contribute to sleep disruption in several ways. Individuals may delay or miss sleep while "partying," the intoxication impairing decisions about the need for sleep. Stimulants actually promote wakefulness and directly compromise the regenerative sleep period. Intoxication can lead to acute illness, such as nausea and vomiting, that disrupts sleep as well. Finally, sedatives, such as alcohol or benzodiazepines, may cause drowsiness but alter sleep patterns and diminish the restorative properties of sleep.

Julio's bedtime beer helped him fall asleep, at least at first, but he never felt good in the morning. It was like he hadn't slept at all.

For some individuals, the combination of multiple contributing factors makes it very difficult to determine what's going on and how best to address the problem. The multitude of reasons for sleep problems after combat deployment demand comprehensive and proactive assessment of sleep quality for veterans and military personnel. We are learning that sleep deprivation from any cause can inhibit the body's ability to regenerate and lowers resiliency across many body systems. Sleep deprivation likely contributes to hypertension, obesity, hormone abnormalities, perpetuation of pain, lowered immunity, and mood disorders.

GULF WAR ILLNESS AND OTHER MEDICALLY UNEXPLAINED SYMPTOMS

Approximately 700,000 U.S. service members were deployed to the Persian Gulf in 1990–1991 for Operation Desert Shield and Operation

Desert Storm. This cohort experienced the suspense-wracked tedium of waiting for the biological and chemical weapons attacks that they were told to anticipate. Frequent alarms signaling possible chemical weapon attacks and having to put on special protective gear reinforced this risk. Eventually, the coalition offensive, led by the United States, was quick and decisive, but despite this success, up to one-third of the deployed troops report ongoing, persistent symptoms that affect their quality of life, much higher than similarly aged civilians or fellow service members who were not deployed to the Gulf. The most commonly reported symptoms include fatigue, widespread achy pain, difficulty with memory and concentration, diarrhea and gastrointestinal distress, and skin problems. Unfortunately, the exact cause and underlying problem that leads to these symptoms is not understood.[11]

Connie just didn't feel right after she returned from the Gulf in 1991. She was tired all the time; her husband, Doug, wouldn't trust her to manage any of their household finances because she couldn't keep the numbers straight; and she wasn't doing well in her job as a nurse supervisor at the local hospital. She also had diarrhea almost every day and a bloating sensation. She had been in really good shape before heading to Kuwait and wondered whether something she was exposed to in the Gulf had ruined her health.

Now in their forties and older, many of the Gulf War veterans continue to report overall health problems that interfere to varying degrees with their ability to function. Managing Gulf War illness is a challenge like a marathon, not a sprint, and since there is no specific treatment for it, chronic disease management strategies are most effective.

Some have proposed that there are chronic, medically unexplained physical symptoms present among deployed troops after every conflict. Recently, the Institute of Medicine, an independent scientific advisory board, has suggested the term "chronic multisymptom illness" to capture the universal nature of this postdeployment phenomenon. Unfortunately, this term is vaguely defined, and cross-era comparison is very difficult. For deployed veterans of non–Gulf War conflicts, the presence of chronic, persistent symptoms should prompt a discussion with a regular health care provider.

HEALTH EFFECTS OF OCCUPATIONAL AND ENVIRONMENTAL EXPOSURES

War is a noisy and dirty business. The circumstances of military training and combat expose personnel to numerous chemicals, harsh environments, unusual diseases, and special medications and vaccines to protect them from these diseases. Even on U.S. soil, military jobs can expose individuals to chemicals with known toxic effects, such as petrochemicals, combustion products, solvents, asbestos, heavy metals, ionizing radiation, and others. Despite the military's best attempts to minimize occupational exposure to known hazards through proper industrial hygiene measures, training and access to personal protective equipment, and monitoring programs, these interventions have not always been in place or completely implemented everywhere. A complete list of possible exposures and their potential health impacts is not possible here, but for certain individuals, occupational or environmental exposure concerns may warrant focused attention.[12]

Gulf War exposures merit special attention given the possible link between Gulf War illness and the highly unusual exposures encountered in 1990–1991 in the Gulf region. Many Gulf War veterans are concerned about a possible "toxic soup" of exposures that might relate to ongoing health problems, including Iraqi chemical weapons (sarin and cyclosarin), pesticides (concentrated DEET and permethrin) used extensively to control insects, smoke from burning oil wells, and prophylactic measures (pyridobromostigmine tablets and vaccines) administered by the U.S. military to protect troops from the possible use of chemical and biological agents by the Iraqis. At this time, there is no recognized definitive cause or causes of Gulf War illnesses. One prominent theory is that a combination of exposures, many of which are suspected to affect function of nerve cells, may have contributed to persistent illness in predisposed individuals.

Agent Orange exposure in Vietnam veterans is another concern of note. Vietnam-era veterans represent more than 7 million of the 23 million U.S. veterans alive. They are also the largest number of veterans currently seeking health care in the Veterans Health Administration. This cohort is over 60 years old, and many are experiencing the common chronic conditions that manifest in older Americans more generally, including cardiovascular disease, hypertension, diabetes, obesity, prostate cancer, and sleep apnea.

Steve didn't do as well as hoped when he got out of the army after Vietnam. He tried going to college but didn't make it past the first semester and took a job at a distribution warehouse. Now 64 years old, he felt that his body was broken down, and he had diabetes and high blood pressure and was very overweight. He kept reading about Agent Orange and wondered if that had anything to do with his health problems.

Concern about Agent Orange, an herbicide used to defoliate the jungle and agricultural areas in Vietnam, is almost unique to Vietnam veterans. Agent Orange was contaminated with dioxin, a known toxin that can cause numerous acute health problems in large enough doses. These include peripheral neuropathy (damage to the nerves going from the spinal cord out to the body) and may contribute to chronic health problems as well, such as cardiovascular disease, cancers, and endocrine abnormalities. There is little direct evidence of these negative outcomes in Vietnam veterans exposed to Agent Orange, but the data about the actual level of exposure for any individual to Agent Orange is very poor. For this reason, any U.S. service member who set foot in Vietnam during the period of conflict is presumed to have come in contact with Agent Orange.

Presuming exposure to Agent Orange, the Department of Veterans Affairs set a policy of service connection for health conditions associated with dioxin. These determinations were made by the Institute of Medicine based on evidence of causal association between dioxin exposure and health complications from other populations and studies of animals. The scientific evidence is reviewed regularly by the Institute of Medicine, and new conclusions are submitted to the Veterans Administration for consideration for updating policy.

SUMMARY

There can be no doubt that war negatively affects the health of combatants. Training and preparation for combat can also put service members in harm's way and result in permanent adverse health effects. The visible and invisible wounds of war don't affect only sexual health, though.

The effects can be long lasting and may interfere with other functioning and engagement with day-to-day activities. While addressing the impact on sexual health is important, getting help is essential to overall functioning and should be sought whenever possible. For each health issue outlined in this chapter, there may be different treatment options; starting with your family physician is a good place to begin the process of healing.

4

EFFECTS OF COMBAT DEPLOYMENT ON SEXUAL HEALTH AND FUNCTION

So how does combat affect sexual health? In chapter 3, we saw how combat can affect health overall. In this chapter, we delve into the specific effects of military service on sexual health and function. This chapter begins with a review of the physiology of the sexual response and then proceeds through many of the same postdeployment health conditions covered in chapter 3 and their impact on sexual health.

Sexual dysfunction is usually not a simple issue. It is almost always a multifactorial challenge because sexual health is affected by a multitude of factors relating to the body, the psyche, and the environment. Employing a biopsychosocial framework, this chapter discusses the primary and secondary impacts of deployment on sexual health, including the effects of sexual dysfunction on relationships and socialization more generally.

PATHOPHYSIOLOGY OF SEXUAL DYSFUNCTION

Remember that sexual function depends on the brain, the peripheral nerves, the correct hormonal balance, and the structural integrity of the genitals and reproductive organs. These biological systems must integrate properly to allow for sexual activity.[1] There are numerous ways that combat experience can disrupt these systems acutely and for the longer term. Some effects may even be permanent, although many are reversible, or compensatory strategies can minimize their impact.

GENITAL INJURIES

Although exact numbers are not readily available, the number of deployed troops who experience physical injuries to their genitals and reproductive organs is not large. For recent veterans of Iraq and Afghanistan, the total number is likely approximately 1,000 to 2,000 out of the more than 2.6 million U.S. troops deployed there since 2001.[2]

For those who are affected, however, structural damage to genitals can require significant adaptation to resume sexual activity. The required adjustments can be determined only at the individual level and usually require iterative learning through trial and error. Pain, discomfort, and imperfect function could be issues even without extensive visible signs of structural damage.

Ted went to his primary care doctor one day very concerned. He had engaged in sex with his girlfriend the night before, and instead of having normal cream-colored semen, it was mixed with bright red blood. They had not been using a condom, and Ted said that his girlfriend freaked out. He remembers it happening one other time while he was masturbating but just put it out of his mind. That episode happened during the first time that his osteomyelitis, a bone infection, flared up in the stump of his amputated leg. He had been feeling a little more tired recently and wondered if the bone infection was coming back again. There had never been any visible damage to his penis or scrotum, but he wondered if there was something wrong on the inside.

He and his primary care doctor discussed how best to determine whether the bone infection was back and what tests to do about the blood in the semen, or hematospermia. They decided to get some blood and urine tests and to seek specialty advice from an infectious disease doctor (for the bone infection) and a urologist (for the hematospermia).

Injury to genitals and reproductive organs can also lead to infertility, another important aspect of sexual health. Infertility could have profound implications for individuals and their partners who are intent on having children.

TRAUMATIC BRAIN INJURY

Traumatic brain injury (TBI) can result in numerous problems that may affect sexual health and functioning. Given the frequency of enemy attacks using improvised explosive devices, rocket-propelled grenades, and other types of explosive munitions resulting in exposure to blast, blast-related TBI has been called the signature wound of the wars in Iraq and Afghanistan. In addition, TBI from direct impact is also common during deployment, happening with motor vehicle accidents, falls, sports and training, and assaults. With moderate and severe TBI, there is often an obvious connection between the damage and sexual health and dysfunction.

David's condition, being minimally responsive to any stimuli, meant he couldn't initiate sexual activity with his wife, and it wasn't clear if he would even be aware of what was happening if she initiated it. This left his wife, Susan, to decide how to maintain her sexual health. She remained incredibly dedicated to her husband's care and well-being and also committed to him as a wife, but at 23 years old, she wondered if she should forgo sexual intimacy with anyone else for the rest of her life or if she had any other options. David wasn't mentally present enough to give her any indication of his thoughts, and they had never talked in advance about anything like this happening. After they had been settled in at home for about a year, she decided she would talk to her mom about these thoughts.

Edward, the 22-year-old young man with a brain injury and serious mobility issues, continued to experience sexual desire. He was able to masturbate and had a strong interest in finding and establishing an intimate relationship with a woman but was struggling to meet women who were interested in him romantically. His mobility and speech issues made him dependent on others, and he felt that this limited his ability to go out and date women. He didn't get a lot of opportunities to meet potential girlfriends, as his time was filled up with medical appointments and therapy, and he didn't want to have his mom take him to a date. He started talking to his buddy about his options.

We are learning that sometimes mild TBI can result in similar if less severe problems. Although most people fully recover from a mild TBI, whether due to a blast or direct impact, it appears that some people develop persistent deficits. With recent research using new imaging techniques and biomarkers, there is a growing awareness of long-lasting damage to the brain in some individuals.[3] Much of the knowledge about the brain and how it contributes to sexual health and function comes from research in animals or by extrapolation from more severe examples of TBI in humans. These results have contributed to our growing knowledge about how the human brain works and governs sexual health, but there is still a lot of uncertainty.[4] Trying to apply the new discoveries to an individual seeking care in a physician's office is still more of an art than a science.

Detecting abnormalities in the brain structures after mild TBI that are related to sexual health or that explain sexual health issues is very challenging. Current clinical methods, such as magnetic resonance imaging (MRI), have the resolution power to detect abnormalities only in groups of brain cells and their supporting structures and connections. Newer MRI methods that are not part of standard clinical practice yet—such as functional MRI, which looks at brain cell function in areas of the brain, and diffusion tensor imaging, which looks at the connections between parts of the brain—also do not have adequate resolution to look at the individual nerve cell circuits that likely form the basis for sexual function.

The brain, especially the hypothalamus and the adjacent pituitary, are essential to the regulation of the body's sex hormones. Certainly for individuals with moderate or severe TBI (and perhaps for some with mild TBI), damage to these structures can result in disruption of the hormonal milieu underlying sexual health. Testosterone, progesterone, oxytocin, estrogen, and other hormones are what determine the level of sexual desire and regulate the likelihood of becoming aroused. Some of these hormones also likely affect the brain's ability to encode new information, that is, modulate memories of past experiences and evolve new preferences about desired partners and activities.

There is some evidence that a portion of service members who experience head injury may develop subtle or even overt abnormalities of the hypothalamic-pituitary-gonadal axis, the hormone loop most directly related to sexual health and function. This hormone loop is directly responsible for levels of testosterone, progesterone, estrogen, and other hormones that regulate human reproduction and sexual health. Women may see their menstrual cycles affected, and men may experience low testosterone with loss of secondary male sex characteristics and difficulty achieving and maintaining an erection. Both men and women can experience a decrease in sexual desire and fertility when this hormone system is affected.

"Joe" described how after he recovered from his head injury, which laid him up for several days with a headache, dizziness, and memory problems, his sexual health has never been the same. He was engaging in sexual relations with his wife three or four times a week before the injury, and afterward he was barely interested, could hardly get an erection, couldn't maintain it long enough for his wife's satisfaction, and was very dissatisfied with the experience. To others, he looked completely "normal," and even his wife was initially confused by his difficulty with sexual intercourse. She wondered if he no longer found her desirable, and eventually she just flat out asked him why he wasn't as interested in sex with her as before.

Measuring and interpreting hormone levels is challenging and often requires the expertise of an endocrinologist, a doctor who specializes in the hormone systems of the body. The secretion of hormones often occurs in a cyclical pattern, such as the monthly cycle of the female reproductive hormones or the daily cycle of cortisol. So the timing of hormone testing is critical. In addition, not all hormone detected in blood samples is active or able to cause an effect. Some is bound to proteins in the blood and becomes available only if other factors in the blood change. Finally, our knowledge of the relationship between hormone levels and other factors, as well, is imprecise. It appears that sudden changes in hormone levels and the levels of one hormone relative to another may often be as important as the absolute hormone levels themselves.[5] This makes interpretation of current laboratory tests for hormones very much an art.

Juan had a severe TBI and suffered from many cognitive, motor (control of body parts), and emotional/behavioral consequences. In addition, he had a low testosterone level and a low free testosterone level (active form of testosterone). He also had diabetes insipidus, an inability to control his water level, and a thyroid problem, both due to hormone deficiencies. Juan occasionally experienced sexual desire and a flicker of an erection but was unable to maintain the erection.

When Juan began talking to his primary care doctor about his lack of interest in sex and inability to get an erection, they began discussing the pros and cons of supplementing his testosterone and how to do this safely and while monitoring his other hormone-based problems. Juan was interested in testosterone supplementation, but the manager of the group home was concerned that his behavior might become more problematic if he were given testosterone. They consulted an endocrinologist (a hormone specialist) who initially said it was probably more harmful than beneficial. With additional discussion between Juan, the primary care doctor, the endocrinologist, a rehabilitation medicine specialist, and his group home providers, the team decided that a short trial of testosterone supplementation would be appropriate. They agreed to monitor his behavior for signs of aggression or inappropriate sexual activity (especially because he lived in a group home) and his testosterone and free testosterone levels and levels of the other deficient hormones, red blood cell measures, and blood chemistries that might be affected by the change in testosterone.

By the third month of the trial with the low dose of testosterone gel applied daily, there were no problems noticed. Juan said that he felt better, had more energy, and noticed that he sometimes woke up in the morning with a partial erection. Since this first dose seemed to help and certainly didn't cause any new problems, the team agreed to try a slightly higher dose with ongoing monitoring.

POLYTRAUMA

Sometimes, veterans have extensive musculoskeletal injuries and dysfunction without brain injury. These conditions can result in significant dependence on others, similar to severe TBI.[6]

Clarissa was confined to a motorized wheelchair outside the house after her back surgery and had limited mobility using a walker while inside the house. She accepted the house rules of her parents even though she had been independent for many years already, stating that she was grateful for their support. She wanted to focus on raising her seven-year-old daughter and continue her physical rehabilitation. She also hadn't been sexually active since her surgery and wasn't sure how she would navigate sexual activity given the weakness in her legs and her urinary incontinence. She wondered how these things would affect the experience for her and her partner, whoever that might be since she wasn't even dating. One day, her friend invited her to a party for the following Friday, and Clarissa's parents agreed to babysit her daughter. Clarissa was thrilled to be going out.

PAIN

For those who experience chronic musculoskeletal pain persistently or episodically over time, the impact on their lives can be dramatic and depressing.[7] Chronic pain can also have direct and indirect negative effects on sexual health.

Jack went to his Veterans Administration primary care physician for the first time about one year after his military health care team did his back surgery for a pinched nerve in his lower spine. He still had a stash of ibuprofen, an anti-inflammatory pain medicine, and hydrocodone, an opioid pain medicine. His new wife, Monica, was very disappointed with his sexual performance after the initial recuperation from the surgery and wanted him to discuss it with his doctor. Jack reported that he was able to engage in sexual activity only while lying on his back; any other position caused back pain that killed his erection and his interest in sex. Reevaluation indicated that there were no detectable problems with the surgery or the hardware and nothing that was amenable to additional surgical intervention. Jack was reassured and engaged more in physical therapy and home-based exercises.

Jack and Monica experimented with other positions and intimate activities. Jack also continued to use the ibuprofen and hydrocodone to manage the pain he still sometimes experienced with sexual activity and other physical activities. Over time, the intensity of the pain decreased.

POSTTRAUMATIC STRESS DISORDER

Posttraumatic stress disorder (PTSD) is associated with sexual dysfunction and may affect sexual health in many ways. Although the exact mechanisms are not fully understood, it is thought that PTSD can directly affect sexual health and function in several ways. First, the sexual response cycle—arousal, maintenance, and climax—is largely under the control of the autonomic system. PTSD is also associated with changes in autonomic function, providing one possible mechanism by which

PTSD can directly impact sexual health. Hormonal changes related to PTSD, although not necessarily in the core set of hormones governing reproduction and sexual health, might disrupt the delicate balance of hormones overall and compromise optimal sexual health. Sexual health and function also require a degree of learning and conscious control; disruptions to learning circuits in the brain from previous trauma may negatively affect sexual health, especially when the PTSD is related to trauma of a sexual nature. Finally, engaging in sexual activity with a partner requires social interaction; you must enter the "market" to meet potential partners, often in public or group settings. The isolating behaviors of PTSD may make this difficult. You also must mutually agree to proceed with an intimate relationship. Achieving this agreement can take negotiation and give-and-take between the partners. Symptoms of PTSD, especially the irritability and quick temper considered part of hyperarousal, can interfere with several of these activities.

PTSD after deployment can result from a wide range of traumas, not all of them directly related to bombing, gunfire, face-to-face fighting, or other "typical" war experiences. Some individuals experience a sense of life-threatening trauma from the isolation and dread of waiting for an attack that might never come. Many individuals deploy with a sense of foreboding that they will never come back. Unfortunately, these feelings can contribute to full-blown PTSD, especially when the service member's unit is dysfunctional or he or she is harassed or assaulted by another U.S. service member. PTSD associated with sexual trauma that occurs during deployment is an important consideration, especially for women service members.

By the time Maria got home after deployment, she was having flashbacks to some of the sexual encounters she was forced to have with her sergeant. She was irritable and withdrawn and avoided contact with men in general. She wasn't able to bring herself to talk about the sexual trauma she experienced while deployed, thinking that people wouldn't believe her and that somehow it was her fault. When her boyfriend tried to reengage her in intimate physical activities, she couldn't tolerate it. She would see the face of that sergeant and become sick to her stomach. She would push her boyfriend away, sometimes violently if he persisted too long in his attempt to love her. While she kind of knew what the problem was, she couldn't help herself from reacting this way. Her heart rate increased, and she just wanted to run away from him.

Her boyfriend tried to help her by asking her what was going on, but she didn't feel safe enough to tell him. After her boyfriend gave up and left her, she had no interest in seeking a new partner; it was like she had never had sex before and wasn't interested in it ever again.

This vignette illustrates several important effects of PTSD on sexual health. First, the hyperarousal of PTSD is not the same as the arousal phase in the sexual response cycle. Maria experienced the hyperarousal symptoms of PTSD that dramatically interfered with her sexual response to her boyfriend's overtures. For veterans for whom the trauma experience is sexual in nature, this aspect of PTSD can make sexual activities incredibly distressing and challenging.[8] Maria also acted in a way that increased her isolation despite knowing that she really needed help to cope with her sexual trauma; she just didn't know whom to ask or where to go for the help.

PTSD can have secondary effects on sexual health by affecting a partner or compromising other life situations that promote sexual health, such as engaging in social or civic organizations or activities.

Tom thought he was doing okay after separating from the military after two deployments to Iraq with the U.S. Marine Corps. He had seen quite a bit of combat firsthand but was happily married to Lisa and working as a police officer. Every year around the anniversary of the Battle of Fallujah, he experienced a recurrent nightmare and would "act out" some of the dream, grabbing Lisa around the neck and choking her. When he awoke, he wouldn't recall any of the dream or the fact that he grabbed her. This petrified her and made him feel awful. They decided that despite their loving relationship and preference for sharing a bed and falling asleep next to each other after sexual intercourse, they would need to sleep in separate beds to ensure Lisa's safety while he sought out additional help for this symptom of PTSD.

After getting into the fight at the veterans' meet-up, Julio couldn't bring himself to try again. He didn't know where to go to meet women he might be interested in. He tried online dating, but even if he found someone he was interested in, it seemed they always wanted to meet at a bar, restaurant, or coffee shop. Being in crowded public places like these made him anxious, and he had difficulty focusing. He would drink alcohol before the dates to help him get through them. The dates never went well because Julio always had to sit with his back to the wall, was always looking around, and seemed very uncomfortable. The women often thought he was rude because they thought he was looking at other women or in trouble, especially if they smelled the alcohol on his breath. He rarely got a second date with the same woman.

Thus, the effects of PTSD on sexual health can be direct or secondary to the social impact of symptoms of PTSD. As discussed in chapter 3, the symptoms of PTSD come and go, and different combinations may be prominent at different times. This variability can also make it hard to manage PTSD as the challenges may vary from day to day. Given the pervasive impact of PTSD and its symptoms, it is critical to optimize its management to maximize sexual health. The best evidence supports a combination of medications to help alleviate the symptoms of PTSD and certain psychotherapies to promote processing the traumatic memories and heal the brain circuits damaged by the experiences.

DEPRESSION

Like PTSD, depression can have a direct or an indirect effect on sexual health. Depression is strongly associated with sexual dysfunction, and lack of sexual desire is often a prominent feature of depression. Suppression of sexual desire is often a direct manifestation of the anhedonia, or general lack of desire, associated with depression that likely reflects changes in brain circuitry and chemistry. Depressed individuals also report difficulty becoming (or even an inability to become) aroused or maintaining arousal or climaxing.

In addition, the social impact of other symptoms of depression can also interfere with sexual health and function in ways that are similar to PTSD. Increased isolation and withdrawal can inhibit social interactions that might lead to new partnerships. Low self-esteem and feelings of guilt can sap the self-confidence necessary to engage and impress new people in a way that might lead to a relationship or sexual activity.

Maria was now single after her boyfriend left her and feeling increasingly low and isolated. Her desire for sexual relations was nonexistent, and her interest in engaging in any social activity was very low. She was beginning to feel that life was not worth living.

The dreaded complication of depression-suicide, although rare, has been associated with military service and deployment in the media and has gained a great deal of attention. Often, relationship problems, although not necessarily the sexual aspect of the relationship, are found to be possible contributing factors to suicide attempts and completions. In retrospect, intimate partners often realize that the challenges in the relationship provided some clue to the depth of suffering experienced by the veteran or service member who completed suicide.

ADVERSE EFFECTS OF MEDICATION

Medicines prescribed to treat depression and PTSD can also impact sexual function. The selective serotonin reuptake inhibitors (SSRIs) are commonly prescribed for veterans with PTSD to help manage symptoms. These medicines are also indicated and prescribed for depression and anxiety. There are several medications in this class with similar effects, although each may have a different effect in a certain individual. These medicines have been available for many decades and are generally considered safe and effective, but they can cause side effects in some people.

The SSRIs are thought to contribute to difficulty with arousal, maintenance, and climax. They likely do so by altering some of the brain circuitry and autonomic nerve function. For men, this is most commonly noted as an inability to achieve orgasm and ejaculation despite satisfactory stimulation. In women, the lack of arousal and anorgasmia can be equally problematic.

Tom was prescribed medication, an SSRI, to help him manage his PTSD symptoms. About a month after starting the medicine, he thought he might have been feeling less irritable but also noticed that he couldn't achieve orgasm when engaging in intercourse with his wife, Lisa. The first time it happened, he faked ejaculating in her vagina after she climaxed, but when it happened a second and third time, he began to wonder what was happening. He felt diminished in his masculinity and reduced his requests for sexual activity with his wife. Lisa in turn wondered what had changed in him, as they had previously joked about how "regular" he was in wanting to be with her and she enjoyed their pattern of sexual activity. She thought perhaps he had found someone else and worried about his having an affair. She also wondered if he found her less desirable for some reason.

In the depths of depression or with out-of-control PTSD symptoms, the side effects of SSRIs might not be as noticeable; the individual has other symptoms and concerns that are more disruptive to sexual and overall health. As the depressed mood starts to lift, however, and sexual desire returns, these adverse effects might become more noticeable. The individual taking the SSRI may now be in the mood occasionally but finds him- or herself having difficulty acting on the desire.

Other medications used to treat PTSD and depression can also have effects on sexual health. Less commonly used for depression today, tricyclic antidepressants are well known to adversely affect arousal. These medications are used at lower doses, however, to help with certain types of nerve pain or to promote sleep. The serotonin-norepinephrine reuptake inhibitors are less likely to contribute to sexual dysfunction than SSRIs but occasionally produce similar side effects.

Certain medicines used to prevent migraines, including beta-blockers (originally a medicine for high blood pressure), can negatively impact arousal, especially erections in men. Less commonly, some of the antiseizure medicines used to prevent migraine headaches or treat certain nerve pain, such as gabapentin, can have similar effects.

As discussed further in chapter 8, it is important to discuss suspected medication side effects with the provider who prescribed the medicine or the primary care provider coordinating your care. Sometimes, it is uncomfortable or even dangerous to suddenly stop a medication. Always consult with a medical professional before making significant changes to your medication use.

SUBSTANCE ABUSE

Substance abuse can have several quite different effects on sexual health and function. Use of depressants, such as alcohol, can impede sexual function, especially at higher doses. Chronic heavy alcohol use can actually lower libido through changes in liver metabolism and resultant imbalance of the circulating and active hormones. Chronic opioid use also changes the hormonal milieu and contributes to hypogonadism, or suppression of testosterone and other hormones. This reduces baseline sexual desire and may interfere with sexual activity as well.

Some types of substance use can seemingly boost sexual activity but often in unhealthy ways. Alcohol in lower quantities reduces inhibitions and can promote social interaction. These effects are often perceived as beneficial and may result in enhanced opportunities to become intimate. Alcohol also begins to impair judgment at about the same dose or quantity that it reduces inhibitions. This can lead to bad choices about which partner to engage with, the use of barrier protection or contraception, particular types of sexual activities or settings, or other behaviors or activities in proximity to the sexual activity.

Clarissa's big night out, the first time since her surgery, finally arrived, and she went to the party at a hotel with her girlfriend. They were having a good time, drinking "a bit," and she "hooked up" with an acquaintance. In the excitement of her first sexual encounter in several years, Clarissa put out of her mind the fact that she wasn't on birth control, they weren't using a condom, and she was in the bedroom adjacent to a living area with eight other people able to hear what was going on. Afterward, her girlfriend helped her back onto her motorized wheelchair, and they went home late that night, Clarissa not feeling well and getting a sinking feeling. The next morning, her phone was an explosion of text messages, including one forwarded from her previous night's partner that said, "I never knew wheelchair sex was so great," enraging her. She called her girlfriend to vent and tried to decide what to do about the possibility of becoming pregnant or contracting a sexually transmitted disease.

Julio was out on a date and had been drinking alcohol at home beforehand, something that he felt would increase his chances of getting through the evening at the bar despite the crowds. The date went well, although he kept drinking, and soon the girl agreed to go back to his place. On the way there, he was very excited and aroused, but when they were making out and getting undressed, he started to lose his erection and was unable to get it back. His partner was very into him and really wanted to go all the way, but Julio became upset at the situation and started to blame her for his loss of erection. She immediately put her clothes on and left, yelling that he wasn't "man enough" for her anyway. As Julio laid down on his bed, he realized he was feeling queasy, and the room was rocking a bit. He fell asleep and woke up late the next morning with a massive headache.

Some stimulants, such as cocaine or methamphetamine, also promote promiscuity, endowing the user with a sense of enhanced sexual prowess while under their influence. These effects are, of course, distorted perceptions of reality that fade as the drug effect wears off. Stimulants also impair judgment and can lead to poor choices. Too often, these drugs lead to physical dependence, craving, and unacceptable behaviors that result in serious social or even legal issues.

SLEEP DISRUPTION

Sleep is essential to the regeneration of the body and processing of sensory input. Sleep deprivation has widespread and profound effects on every body system, especially the ability to think and remember (brain function), the immune system, the cardiovascular system, and the endocrine system. Chronic sleep deprivation contributes to fatigue, obesity, diabetes, high blood pressure, vulnerability to infections, poor mood, pain, and a general feeling of not being well.

A lack of sleep can have a profound impact on libido and the sexual response. Being tired is not conducive to sexual activity. In addition, it is apparent that several body systems that are adversely affected by chronic sleep deprivation are strongly associated with sexual health. Once again, we see that disruption of the hormonal balance from sleep disturbances might be problematic for sexual desire and arousal. The long-term consequences of high blood pressure, cardiovascular disease, diabetes, and obesity may also contribute to diminished sexual health and dysfunction.

Poor mood and difficulty thinking and remembering from persistent sleep disruption can interfere with the social interactions that set up a healthy sex life and contribute to opportunities for sexual activity. With prolonged sleep disturbance, these disturbances may start to look more and more like depression and result in withdrawal from social interactions and more severe suppression of sexual desire.

GULF WAR ILLNESS AND CHRONIC MULTISYMPTOM ILLNESS

The sexual health of Gulf War veterans is not well described in the scientific literature. Anecdotally, a proportion of the more seriously ill Gulf War veterans experience loss of libido and sexual dysfunction related to their fatigue and chronic pain. A few men and women have reported a complete loss of sensation in the genitals or a profound inability to become sexually aroused. They report the tremendous impact of this on their relationships and overall sexual health. These observations are not necessarily unique to Gulf War veterans, however, and, without more definitive research, it is difficult to determine if there is something unique about sexual dysfunction in Gulf War veterans.

Prior to her deployment, Connie enjoyed sexual intimacy with her husband. Her reintegration was especially rocky, and she just wasn't feeling quite right since her deployment. She was always tired and sometimes had a hard time focusing or remembering things. The few times she and her husband, Doug, tried to engage in intimate physical contact, she found it uncomfortable when his penis entered her vagina. At first, she would wait it out but never climaxed herself. Then his entry became more painful, and she started putting up roadblocks to prevent Doug from initiating sexual activity. She didn't feel comfortable talking to him about it and was so tired that she wasn't that interested in sexual activity anyway.

There is even less information available about the impact of the more general chronic multisymptom illness on sexual health and function in veterans of other conflicts. For veterans of Iraq and Afghanistan with chronic multisymptom illness and concerns about sexual health, at this point a one-on-one conversation with a primary care provider is probably the best place to get more information.

AGENT ORANGE EXPOSURE

The sexual health of Vietnam veterans has changed as they've aged and accumulated common chronic diseases like many Americans in their age cohort. For Vietnam veterans, changes in sexual health and sexual activity are most likely a result of normal aging processes (see chapter 6), but some might wonder if Agent Orange has also contributed to their challenges. As discussed in chapter 3, the Veterans Administration has granted presumptive service connection for some health conditions in Vietnam veterans, but these decisions are often based on indirect and incomplete scientific evidence. The overall policy effect is meant to promote access and to ameliorate financial stressors for veterans with conditions possibly related to their deployment to Vietnam.

Cardiovascular disease and diabetes are two presumptive service-connected conditions, and sexual dysfunction is associated with both of these conditions, as is hypertension. Similarly, prostate cancer is a presumptive service-connected condition, and treatment for it can create dramatic sexual health complications and directly contribute to sexual dysfunction through posttreatment nerve or other structural damage. Although this might appear to create an indirect link between exposure to Agent Orange during deployment to Vietnam and a sexual health problem, there is no established direct link, and sexual dysfunction is currently not among the presumed service-connected conditions for Vietnam veterans.

PERSONALITY CHANGES

Some veterans and their families report that they are just different after deployment. Combat and other experiences offer new perspectives and challenge previously held beliefs about what is important. For some veterans, big metaphysical questions are reopened. They wonder about their purpose in life and relationship to others. Combat can affect one's spirituality and core beliefs about humanity.

As Jonah said when asked about the effect of the military on his sexual health in a moment of serious contemplation, "I don't know. I never really thought about it. I guess it was just the stuff I saw there [in Iraq]. It changed me. I'm just not as interested in sex."

SUMMARY

In any individual, it is often hard to pinpoint exactly what experience in the military contributed to sexual health, but most would acknowledge at least a subtle role. In some cases, military or combat experience has had a profound effect on some aspect of their sexual health, and sexual dysfunction can be at least partially attributed to a specific event or deployment-related health issue. Specific health outcomes of combat can certainly interfere with "normal" sexual function, but seeking help for sexual dysfunction can and should be one aspect of healing from the wounds of war. In chapter 8, we discuss more specifics about how to find assistance with sexual health issues due to deployment.

5

DIFFERENT IMPACT OF MILITARY SERVICE ON MEN AND WOMEN

MEN AND WOMEN ARE DIFFERENT

Most of the time, it is obvious that men and women are different. The human species is essentially sexually dimorphic, meaning that there are two sexual types of anatomy and physiology, although there are a few, rare in-between variations as well. This is because our genetic makeup (the presence of two X chromosomes [XX, women] or one X and one Y chromosome [XY, men]) determines whether we develop male or female body structures. As described in chapter 1, the differences in the genitals and reproductive organs between men and women develop from common cell clusters, which can be considered paired even in maturity. For example, the ovaries and testes are the "equivalent" organs in women and men. They are derived from protogonads present in the same location in very early genetically male (XY) and female (XX) fetuses. The differences that accumulate through development are programmed by the genes and expressed over the life span of the individual. Many factors can influence how the differences between men and women become apparent.

At least partly because of the differences in anatomy and physiology between men and women, military experiences and culture can affect men and women and their sexual health and function differently. This chapter explores how military experience can have different impacts on the sexual health and function of men and women.

Differences in Body Structure

The divergence in genitals and other reproductive organs and parts of the nervous and endocrine systems that control them happens continuously during fetal development and throughout life. Think of puberty and the development of secondary sex characteristics, such as body hair and breast development. Similarly, differences in behaviors and preferences become more pronounced as sexual awareness grows and the individual begins experimenting with sexual activity. Pregnancy and lactation produce additional changes to the woman's body. Eventually, changing hormone levels lead to menopause in women and andropause in men, perhaps creating slight convergence in the hormonal milieu of men and women at that point but not erasing the differences that have accumulated and intensified over their lives.[1]

The differences between men and women have profound and fundamental implications for sexual health and function. Once again, structure plays an important role. Men and women are historically defined by their different external genitals (women: vulva and vagina; men: penis and scrotum), making some sexual roles and activities possible and others more difficult or impossible. Widely divergent reproductive organs (women: ovaries and uterus; men: testes) result in very different roles for men and women in reproduction. There are also other body structure differences between the sexes related to height, body composition, body and scalp hair distributions, breast tissue, bone structure, and muscle mass. These contribute to differences in sexual health and function primarily as visible markers of human sexual dimorphism.

Hormone Differences

Men and women have different hormones as well. The differences in the levels and balance of hormones certainly play a role in the different preferences that men and women have for the amount and type of sexual activity, partners, and probably the relative importance and role of sexual activity in the context of broader life activities. Women usually have a pronounced, regular monthly cycle of hormone changes (follicle-stimulating hormone, luteinizing hormone, estrogen, estradiol, and progesterone) controlling development and release of fertile eggs, preparation of the uterus and cervix, menses, and even interest in sexual activity and preference for different "types" of partners. Men also have a monthly hormone cycle, but it is not nearly as apparent and is generally not considered clinically relevant in usual health.

Testosterone level is probably related to baseline desire for sexual activity in both men and women; men have higher levels than women. Supplementing low testosterone in men clearly increases self-reported interest and engagement in sexual activity. This is less prominent but possibly true in women as well. Testosterone also plays a major role in the secondary sex characteristics, and too much testosterone in women can have an androgenizing effect, causing male features, such as body hair and male-pattern baldness, to become more pronounced.

Oxytocin, a hormone released from the brain, is critical for lactation in women and is increasingly appreciated as important in creating and strengthening interpersonal relationships in both men and women. The differences between levels and functions of oxytocin in men and women are still being clarified, but they likely color differences in perceptions of sexual health and functioning between men and women as well.

The differences in the hormonal milieu are likely among the most important drivers of different behaviors, attitudes, and beliefs between men and women. As scientists uncover more details about how hormones interact and cause changes at the cellular level, clinicians may become more able to help patients optimize their sexual health at the root of the action.

Reiterating the Similarities between Men and Women

There are several important observations to make about the differences among men and women before progressing further into the different effects of military experience on the sexes. First, men and women do belong to the same species and in many respects are more similar than they are different. For example, both sexes are generally interested in sexual health and activity. This pertains to sexual activity related to and separate from desire to procreate. The perceived costs and benefits of seeking sexual activity and preferences for type and frequency of sexual activity may differ on average between men and women, but the biologic drive to engage in sex is present in both sexes. In fact, the ranges of interest in sexual activity for men and women overlap significantly, with some women being more highly interested than some men and vice versa.

Second, sexual health is not just about sexual intercourse, and this is true for both men and women. There is a variety of behaviors and activities that come under the rubric of sexual activity, and the preference for these varies more by individual than by men versus women. In other words, specific sexual activities, such as teasing, joking with sexual innuendo, kissing, stimulating the nipples, petting genitals, or oral sex, may be attractive to one man or woman but not another. Similarly, there is a wide range of preferences for a type of partner; think of any human characteristic, such as tall, skinny, funny, serious, and you can think of both men and women who would find that an attractive trait. It is true that the majority of women prefer a male partner and vice versa, but there is a recognizable minority of people who prefer same-sex partners or may not express a firm preference for a partner of one sex or the other. It is very difficult to generalize about an individual's preferences in partner attributes based on sex alone.

Finally, sexual health is but one domain in the overall health of any individual, man or woman. For many, it is not necessarily the most important domain, and the priority given to sexual activity may vary dramatically over the life span of the person (see chapter 6 for more detailed discussion). Chronic health conditions, acute health issues, psychological stress, or social situations often exert tremendous influence over sexual health and especially sexual activity. The relative importance of competing issues may differ between men and women on average, but the need to prioritize sexual health issues in the overall context of one's life is universal.

DIFFERENT IMPACT OF MILITARY SERVICE ON MEN AND WOMEN

As covered in chapter 2, there are many historical and cultural factors in the military that might contribute to sexual health effects and function. Some of these factors may have different effects on men compared to women. In previous chapters, we explored the effects of deployment on health overall (chapter 3) and sexual health more specifically (chapter 4). Because men and women are different and have different experiences in the military, the prevalence and impact of these effects on sexual health may also differ between men and women.

Differential Impact of Physical Environment during Deployment

Historically, women were not deployed to combat. Starting in the Korean conflict and increasingly common ever since, women have been deployed to combat theaters in noncombat support roles. In 2013, the policy changed, and the ability of women service members to serve in combat roles was expanded. The implementation of this policy change is still in progress, and it will likely be several years before its impact is truly recognized.[2]

Given the relatively few number of women deployed (approximately 12 percent of all troops in Iraq or Afghanistan since 2001, the highest of any U.S. deployment ever), women may have to adapt or make do with the available options.[3] For example, equipment, such as body armor or weapons, is often not designed for the typically smaller and differently shaped frame of women. This can lead to higher rates of overuse or traumatic musculoskeletal injuries during training or operations due to suboptimal fit. Also, the rarity of women in the military can lead to fewer facilities for women only, as is the standard in American culture. Women service members may find themselves in locations that don't have separate shower facilities, toilets, or sleeping quarters. This varies tremendously from place to place and has clearly evolved as the role and dispersion of women has increased over the past 50 years. The lack of facilities is most apparent in remote locations where the U.S. military has a small or temporary presence and while on the move.

Rhonda was a marine sergeant deployed to Iraq who led a unit of all men, an unusual situation. After coming home, Rhonda described how her experience was different from her male peers for "many little reasons." For example, the men had no problem taking a roadside break and emptying their bladders behind the trucks while still fairly able to remain aware of their surroundings. She, on the other hand, had to squat near the truck and asked her men to stand a few yards away from the truck facing away from her to ensure her privacy and retain her sense of authority.

Ability to maintain personal hygiene is often very poor for both men and women while deployed, although this too varies by location, unit assignment, and timing of deployment. Showers are often jerry-rigged in less established outposts, and troops routinely go days without an opportunity to clean up. For women, poor hygiene can contribute to the development of vaginal yeast infections and urinary tract infections. Women are more likely than men, in general, to develop urinary tract infections, and the deprivations of combat deployment increase their risk for these. Vaginal yeast infections can be very uncomfortable, although they do not usually lead to more serious complications. Urinary tract infections, on the other hand, cause discomfort and can lead to very serious problems if not treated.

Connie served as a nurse in the Gulf War in 1991. She recalled being on duty almost constantly for five days around the time of the ground war. She got a little dehydrated and realized she hadn't voided for almost an entire day. She hadn't showered in two days at that point. She finally used the toilet and recognized the slight burn of a developing urinary tract infection. She was called back to the triage area, however, and it was almost 12 hours later before she realized that she was getting nauseous, had an uncomfortable cramping sensation in her pelvis, and was light-headed. She almost collapsed and was told to rest on a gurney and receive intravenous fluids. Once she was hydrated again, she could provide a urine sample, which was cloudy and foul smelling. She was treated with antibiotics for a urinary tract infection and told to rest for another 24 hours before returning to duty.

For women with a menstrual cycle, ensuring access to and ability to employ tampons or pads while deployed can be challenging, especially for those moving around a lot. Also, for many women, the stress of deployment may contribute to irregularity in the menstrual cycle, making the timing of menses more difficult to predict. For this reason, many women opt for long-lasting contraceptives, such as a time-release injection in the arm or buttock, or take oral contraceptive pills continuously to suppress their periods.

Rhonda just laughed when asked how she managed her periods during deployment. "You know that row of birth control pills that's a different color? I never took those the whole time I was deployed." She just didn't want to deal with a period, and many doctors feel this is a safe method of contraception for all women.

Properly managed, these issues would be unlikely to contribute to any long-term negative impacts on sexual health or function. The memory of these sexual health concerns and the gaps in structures and services to address them could color the long-term perception of military service for some women, however. Women may also bond over these shared experiences and privations, creating a tighter-knit community with which to share and discuss sexual health issues. In subtle ways like this, military experience can impact longer-term sexual health differently for women and men.

Differential Impact of Role during Deployment

Women service members are often also differentiated from their male colleagues during deployment by their assignments. In addition to the standard noncombat support roles that men also performed (health care, refueling, and supply unit) in Iraq and Afghanistan, women were often assigned to jobs that involved interacting with the local communities, especially the women of the community. Given the mainly Muslim culture with stricter norms about roles for women and interactions between nonrelated men and women, women service members were often called on to act as "cultural ambassadors" to build rapport and elicit intelligence from the local women.

Laurie was out in the local communities several times a week during her deployment. She, her translator, and a guard would go into the villages and talk to the women, trying to build goodwill and gather information about local involvement in fighting. Twice she found herself in hostile situations, but they were able to get out before any fighting broke out. While she knew her work was important and valued, she also saw how she was sidelined when her male peers would start planning the missions with higher risk of fighting. She never heard any disparaging comments about her lack of involvement in the dangerous combat activities, but she suspected that it negatively impacted others' perceptions of her. To compensate, she would act more assertively in meetings and was merciless when others made mistakes. She was respected because she stuck to the rules but also became known as a "hard-ass."

Taken together, these examples highlight some of the sex differences in the deployment experience. They also indicate how women service members might be noticed and the sex differences accentuated for them and their male colleagues and superiors.[4] The compensatory traits and strategies, while perhaps successful in this particular context, may not be as effective in a civilian setting, especially during dating or within a relationship. The characteristics of the individual can be distorted to accommodate the military setting and culture, and these same characteristics may compromise the sexual health of that individual after deployment or separation from the military.

Differential Impact of Separation during Deployment

Traditionally, male service members who were married were deployed while their civilian wives maintained their household associated with the routine of a military base (active duty) or in a civilian community (National Guard or reserves). Often, wives were supported by each other or other female friends and family members until the husband returned. In many households, the division of labor between spouses during the deployment period was not so different from the division of labor even while the husband was in garrison. The wife ran the house, and the husband worked outside the home.

More recently, women service members are deploying with almost the same likelihood as male colleagues. Deployment can create different types of disruption in the regular habits and circumstances of male and female service members. While there may be more sharing of household responsibilities today, many couples continue to divide the work, and women still tend to take primary ownership of child care, cooking, and home care activities. Women service members may also be more likely to be responsible for the care of sick or elderly parents or other relatives. When a mom deploys, ensuring that the partner and other supporters are ready to take on these responsibilities can be especially anxiety provoking and challenging. This is a significant shift from the traditional deployment patterns of earlier conflicts.

The separation of deployment often lasted 12 to 18 months for veterans of Iraq and Afghanistan. This is clearly long enough to stress relationships and promote adaptive approaches to find alternative outlets for sexual activity. Accordingly, the phenomenon of the "Dear John" letter has seen a resurgence in military culture. This refers to the notification by a stateside partner to the deployed service member that their relationship is over. For veterans of the conflicts in Iraq and Afghanistan, marital infidelities and disruption are a common problem. While not always a fatal blow to an established partnership, sexual activity outside the primary relationship is often a dire challenge, especially if discovered while one partner is still deployed. Most often viewed as a breach of trust, infidelity can have a long-lasting impact on the perceptions and behaviors of the affected partners, including sexual behaviors, interest, and function.

About a year after Tom returned home from Iraq, he found some notes addressed to his wife at the bottom of her drawer. There were no dates, but they talked about some details of sexual encounters and were signed by Ruben. Tom confronted Lisa, who initially denied knowing anything about the notes but later admitted that she had a series of dates with Ruben, a work colleague, while Tom was deployed. She insisted that it was over and that she had no contact with him since Tom returned. Enraged, Tom left the house and didn't return for a few days, staying with a friend while he cooled off. He and Lisa decided to try to work things out rather than breaking it off right then.

SEXUAL ACTIVITY AND SEX-BASED DIFFERENTIAL STIGMA

The limits of socially acceptable sexual activity are different for men and women in many cultures. As in the broader U.S. society, there is a perception among some members of the military community that frequent, casual sexual activity by a single man is a sign of virility and desirability. This behavior can mark him as a standout among his peers. Less frequently discussed sexual activities, such as experimentation with different positions, group sex, oral or anal sex, and use of sex toys, may also be considered by some as marks of virility or an adventurous sexual appetite in a man. Public awareness of similar activity by a woman service member, however, would be more likely to lead to a pejorative label and might cause others to avoid socializing with her due to the stigma of her sexual activities. In some cases, it may cause others to treat her differently, to pursue her for sexual activities, or to harass her for her "reputation." In many ways, a traditional mentality still applies.

Mark was known for his sexual adventures and uninhibited approach to life. He had been enlisted in the navy for 19 years and thoroughly enjoyed his cruises. He knew all the fun places to hang out and meet attractive and available local women, and the younger seamen would often join him on shore leave. Mark enjoyed showing the younger guys the ropes and just didn't bother to tell anyone that he was married.

A clear example of different social standards for individuals based primarily on sex, the stigma of casual or promiscuous sexual activity for women service members is likely both a symptom of rigid cultural norms for a woman's role and behavior and a factor in the depersonalization of women service members. Once again, adapting to these expectations and norms can be harmful to the sexual health of men and women once they leave the military setting.

Jonah, a marine, summed up his opinion of women in the Marine Corps. "I wouldn't touch a female marine for any amount of money. They all sleep around; they're all sluts. Why else would they end up in the Marine Corps? And if they weren't like that before, they probably are now."

By denigrating women who engage in casual sex and lumping them into a single inferior class with the use of demeaning labels, women service members may lose their individual identities. Instead of "Suzie, the blonde woman from Arkansas who works at the commissary," she just becomes "the blonde chick," a label, a name, a reputation. This depersonalization could contribute to a perception among some service members that turns women into relatively faceless, easier targets for sexual violence. Living every day in a culture with second-class status can also contribute to internalized thoughts of "perhaps I really am inferior." These can color one's perceptions, sexual health, and sexual function for a long time to follow.

Not Conforming to Military Cultural Expectations

Military culture is very heterogeneous, not a uniform set of rules and norms as it may appear at first. There are numerous "subcultures" as well and great tolerance for individual differences within the military overall. As discussed in chapter 2, however, there is a prevalent stereotype of masculinity about men in the military and several historical reasons and even current policies that reinforce this image of men. This is demonstrated through the importance of optimizing physical fitness and body image with regular exercise to achieve an ideal masculine appearance.[5] Socialization at the unit level can also reinforce expectations, testing the boundaries of what's acceptable and what is not.

Jack recounted how the guys in his all-male unit would sit around during downtime on the forward operating base, making comments and playing pranks trying to "out-gay" each other. The goal was to say something or simulate an activity or behavior ever more outrageous to provoke a unified response of "disgust" from the others. It was also a test to see who would be sensitive to the raunchy content. Those who failed the test by indicating embarrassment would often be teased because of their reaction. Jack just expected others to behave this way, and when his humor became a little off-color at work after he separated from the military, he was considered insensitive and inappropriate by several of his workmates. It took a while for him to realize why he was not included in some of the after-work social events. This especially irked him when they hired a new, attractive young woman in the office and he found out he wasn't invited to the happy-hour welcome party they had for her.

For male service members who do not "fit" the stereotype regardless of their actual sexual orientation or experiences, life can be challenging especially for enlisted and at the lower ranks.

Jonah did not like the immature behavior of many of the other guys in his unit. He preferred to do his own thing, and when he told off his roommate for snooping around his things, word got around that he was hiding gay porn in his rucksack. Completely false, this rumor caused Jonah a great deal of frustration and hassle. He became even more private and really didn't have any friends in his unit.

Women, with the implied double standard of needing accommodations based on sex but striving to excel in this mainly masculine culture, may experience less stigma or barriers when acting more masculine. Women who adopt more traits and attitudes culturally categorized as male—including, for example, striving for greater physical strength, eating larger quantities of food, laughing at deprivation, and engaging in raunchy humor—are perhaps more likely to find acceptance than a male service member who displays traits or attitudes considered effeminate. However, this relative acceptance of masculine traits may not extend completely to homosexual orientation or activity in women service members given recent policies and still-prevalent attitudes about homosexuality.

Laurie, a recently retired officer known for her direct and no-nonsense manner, laughed about missing the Super Bowl. "I guess I had to take my 'man card' down for the evening. I watched *Downton Abbey*, instead." Her male colleagues, also former military, laughed and reassured her that she was "still okay on that front." Her colleagues without military experience didn't get what the big deal was or why she wanted to have a "man card" in the first place.

These subtle and overt experiences influence self-perception and behavior that can impact sexual health and function. While service members may create an identity that is very acceptable and contributes to their success in the military, the same image and associated behaviors may create challenges or even be dysfunctional in a civilian setting.

Steve, a Vietnam veteran in his late sixties, was on his fourth marriage with four grown children, this time to a woman from the Philippines he met through a magazine ad. When Steve lost his job in his thirties, his second wife went back to being a teacher's aide thanks to her network of family and friends, and Steve found himself floundering. Steve was pretty fixed in his ways and couldn't tolerate his wife taking charge or earning more than him. His continued insistence that she take care of the house and kids led to increasing resentment until she left him, and he retained the right to visit the kids only on weekends and some holidays. Commenting on his impending marriage to his fourth wife, he said, "This time I got it right. She'll do whatever I tell her to, just the way it should be."

Perpetuation of attitudes and behaviors related to sex and roles that are successful in the military can contribute to lifelong challenges and dysfunction. Many service members adapt to their new settings, but some do not and or may only partially do so. Failure to adapt can result in isolation, dysfunctional relationships, or broken relationships and compromise the sexual health of the service member or veteran.

Sex-Based Differences with Sexual Trauma

Sexual trauma is much more prevalent among women service members than among men. While acknowledging undercounting and different definitions of sexual trauma, estimates of experiencing sexual trauma range from 15 to 50 percent of all women service members.[6] An area of intense general media interest, namely, sexual assault directed toward women service members, is clearly related to several factors, including the much larger number of men compared to women service members, the predominance of heterosexual preferences, the differences in perceived roles and status of men and women in the military, broader cultural factors contributing to violence against women, and perhaps an element of increased risk of victimization among women who join the military due to a history of early life abuse.

Given the male-to-female ratio of approximately nine to one in the military overall, chances are greater that sexual assault will be committed by a man. Given a greater than 90 percent rate of heterosexual preference, the target of sexual violence by a male service member will most likely be a woman. Since sexual violence is not just about—and is sometimes not at all about—sexual desire, other factors also contribute to the female predominance as victims of sexual trauma.

As alluded to above, military culture can be perceived by some as placing women overall in a second-class status by highlighting differences between men and women service members. The differences can be exaggerated for the sake of argument, as generally weaker, smaller women are relegated to noncombat support and communications, health care, and intelligence roles not because that's the best fit for their valuable skills and attributes but rather because they are failures. The sex differences as emphasized and perpetuated by the military may be perceived by some as limitations or weaknesses preventing full achievement of the ultimate goal in military service: being a warrior, a killer. For the sexual violence perpetrator, finding a vulnerable potential victim, perhaps someone with a victim-like demeanor (learned from previous experience with abuse), may be challenging given the relatively few women in the military. Finding and cultivating opportunities to act, on the other hand, may be relatively easy within the hierarchical structure and nonquestioning military culture that may seem to the perpetrator to devalue women service members.

Men, while much less likely to experience sexual assault while in the military (estimated rates are less than 5 percent of male service members),[7] may face greater perceived stigma if the experience becomes public. Data are hard to come by, but most sexual trauma against men is committed by other men, and often neither party identifies as homosexual. This reinforces the fact that sexual violence and harassment are often not about sexual desire. These cases are more often about establishing dominance through creating a shared, secret knowledge of an episode of sexual domination that the victim is ashamed to disclose to anyone. In the masculine military culture, being subjected involuntarily to sexual contact with another man may be construed by many as a humiliation striking at the core of a man's identity.

Jonah remembered the first sergeant from his unit at Camp Pendleton. The guy just didn't like him. Whatever Jonah did, it was wrong or not good enough. Occasionally, the first sergeant would get a little pushy, but Jonah wouldn't push back, knowing that could be serious trouble. One day, the first sergeant squeezed Jonah's buttock when Jonah was walking by. Jonah turned around quickly and almost hit him before he realized who did it. From then until he switched units, that first sergeant would goose him whenever he could get away with it, trying to get a rise out of Jonah. Jonah hated this, hated the first sergeant, but didn't dare say anything to anyone. He felt it was humiliating and demoralizing and made him really angry.

The impact of sexual assault or harassment on the sexual health of the victim ranges from no effect to an overwhelming effect. Numerous factors operate in how sexual trauma affects an individual's life: the type and intensity of the trauma, the setting and response to the trauma, social support, previous trauma, and individual resilience, to name a few. After sexual trauma, every aspect of sexual health and function can be impaired: desire, arousal, maintenance, and climax. The memory of the trauma can intrude at any phase and suppress previously normal desires. Even when desire is present and leads to an attempt at sexual activity, arousal may become challenging, especially with more severe sexual trauma, because the physiologic arousal response may serve as a trigger for the traumatic memories. There is also the psychological factor that can affect sexual health behaviors, such as dating. An individual may not trust others enough to explore potential partnerships or may have feelings of worthlessness or even guilt subsequent to the trauma. Wondering "why me?" may lead to negative thoughts that significantly interfere with social interactions moving forward.

Of course, some victims of sexual trauma appear to move on without any apparent effect on their sexual or overall health. Others may react by engaging in promiscuous or reckless sexual activity. As with all human behavior, there is a range of reactions to sexual trauma, and it is important to gain insight into the particular circumstances in each case.

Maria could not keep the images of her sexual trauma from her mind. She kept wondering why she couldn't have prevented it, why she didn't see it coming. Every man she saw was a potential violator, and she couldn't even begin to think about dating someone. On the few occasions she tried to be intimate with her boyfriend, instead of becoming sexually excited, she would get sick to her stomach. That made her feel even worse because she loved her boyfriend and knew he loved her. She didn't know how to get help because she was afraid to tell anyone about what happened. As her sister saw her withdrawing more and more, she finally asked Maria directly if something happened to her. Maria nodded.

SUMMARY

Military life and deployment can affect the sexual health and function of men and women differently, although many of these differences are created indirectly through the reinforcement of cultural norms and expectations and how the individual adapts to these influences. Many of these different effects are likely felt most strongly in the short term, especially during deployment. Some differences in the military experience of men and women service members may have lingering effects or contribute to long-term sexual health issues and dysfunction, although perhaps in subtle ways.

6

THE UPS AND DOWNS
OF SEXUAL HEALTH

Sexual health and function change over the life of an individual. At any age, thoughts, attitudes, beliefs, and behaviors can be recognized as related to sexual health. As children approach puberty and develop secondary sexual characteristics and full reproductive capabilities, their behaviors begin to reflect activities that would promote partnering to satisfy sexual desires, procreation, and child rearing.

Sexual activity in most Americans starts sometime in the teens or twenties, usually a bit earlier for men than women. The frequency of engaging in sexual activity usually peaks for men in the early twenties and for women is a bit closer to 30 years old.[1] This peak coincides with childbearing in many heterosexual couples. Sexual health is about more than procreation, however, and sexual activity continues for most people until late in life, although the frequency, type, and satisfaction with sexual activity all change with aging.

PREMILITARY SEXUAL HEALTH

When the draft was in force, a reality for Vietnam veterans and those of prior conflicts, young men were selected to join the military at age 18. With the all-volunteer force of the U.S. military since the 1970s, people today make a choice to join the military. Most still join at a young age, however, often prior to 20 years old. While most Americans have prob-

ably engaged in some sexual activity by this age, the amount of experience with relationships and life in general may be quite limited. For
many of the young, new military personnel, they have known only their
parents' home, school, and perhaps part-time work. Joining the military
is a major life event at any age, and with limited experience to serve as a
frame of reference, most new military personnel struggle to make sense
of it all.

Eric was a deferred entry army recruit who enlisted at age 17 while
still in high school and shipped off to boot camp in August after gradua-
tion. He still didn't have enough facial hair to shave regularly and had
never had a steady girlfriend. His father and uncles were in the military,
so he was enthusiastic about enlisting, but the day of his departure, his
travel orders were messed up, and he ended up on a flight by himself.
Sitting next to a dad and his twin five-year-old boys, Eric became teary
eyed when relating that this was his first flight and his second overnight
trip from home and that he really had no idea what was in store for him.

For many, joining the military represents the largest, if not the first,
life change of their lives to that point. The young recruit must negotiate
the new situation, meeting new people and learning the rules and expectations of the military. These challenges are present with regard to
sexual health and function as well, and given the relative inexperience
of most young adults on their entry to the military, the focus should be
on exploring options and learning and making decisions that promote
sexual and overall health, not just generate pleasure for the short term.
Preparing for military service, including exposure to information about
the rules of engaging in relationships and sexual activity, would be very
helpful to most recruits.

SEXUAL HEALTH DURING MILITARY SERVICE: AGES 18 TO 30

The military population consists largely of men and women in their late
teens and twenties, coinciding with the peak sexual activity for men and
women and a critical juncture for establishing a core, stable identity in
general as well as solidifying one's sexuality. This timing has several
implications, the important one being that these young men and women
are looking for partners and sexual activity. The military has strict rules

in the form of policies and practices to provide formal guidance about sexual activities and sexuality, as noted in chapter 2. The application of these policies and practices has a significant impact on the sexual health of service members and veterans, as discussed extensively in chapter 4.

Mark, now 37 years old, had been married his entire 19 years of navy service. At first, he was faithful to his wife, Mary, but by his mid-twenties, as their interests diverged and he reenlisted and continued to spend months away at sea, he began to explore other outlets for sexual activity. He justified it to himself that he was still young and attractive and shouldn't have to suppress his desires as long as he was careful. There would be plenty of time for growing old together with his wife—or so he thought.

Of course, now that Mark was approaching his retirement from the navy, the prospect of settling down with his wife and teenage kids seemed foreign to him. Mary didn't seem so keen to have him around all the time, either. He wondered how they would make this work and, in retrospect, whether he should've been more attentive to his home life.

Prior to deployment and while still single and newly turned 21 years old, Jack would enjoy his occasional weekend off by driving about an hour from base and renting a hotel room with a buddy. They would hit the local clubs and try to pick up young women to bring back to their hotel for the night. There was always plenty of alcohol to go around, and usually everyone had a good time. He enjoyed the casual sex and had many different partners in the months before he was deployed.

Tom and Lisa got married right after Tom finished boot camp at age 20. They lived together off base for the next four years. When he wasn't deployed, living off base was a pretty good situation for them. They had some privacy in their apartment but could take advantage of the supportive programs on the base. They had their first child toward the end of that four-year period. They had found the optimal sexual health for both of them and their relationship.

A corollary of the timing of typical military service for aging and sexual health is that men and women may enter the military perceiving themselves at the pinnacle of their sexual health. Indeed, most people joining the military in recent times are at their top physical health overall, required to pass rigorous health and fitness standards before being accepted. Entering the military, experiencing the ups and downs of its culture and activities, and then separating four, six, eight, or 10 years later, individuals may look back and notice a marked decrease in their overall physical and sexual health. This decrease may be completely independent of their military service; that is, they might have experienced the same change if they had taken a civilian job instead of entering the military. But the human mind tends to draw connections to make sense of the world, and often people will attribute changes to something without actual evidence of a causal relationship. Some former military service members and their family may wonder if something they experienced during service caused the change.

As Jonah said, "I guess it was just the stuff I saw there [in Iraq]. It changed me. I'm just not as interested in sex."

It is true that for some people, there is more than just the timing supporting a link between military service and decline in sexual health and function. As mentioned in previous chapters, there are numerous ways in which military service can impact sexual health and function, and sometimes events are clearly linked to problems. More often, however, the link is more subtle, and a decrease in the frequency of and satisfaction with sexual activity may be merely a reflection of how the natural aging process and changing life roles and responsibilities alter one's sexual health and sexuality.

SHORT-TERM DECLINES IN SEXUAL HEALTH

Sexual health also varies within shorter time spans because sexual health is a component of overall health. Just as overall health suffers in the presence of physical, social, or psychological stressors, sexual health suffers as well. Given the linkage between sexual health and reproduction, in times of stress or deprivation, desire for sex is diminished or suppressed. Being sick with a cold or flu usually kills the desire for sexual activity in most individuals. Some activities during military service, especially strenuous trainings such as boot camp or special operations training and deployment to combat and other harsh settings, can shut down interest in sexual activity and inhibit the sexual response cycle. This is accomplished at multiple points in the complex system of brain, nerves, hormones, and genitals as resources are directed by the body to more immediately important functions. Usually, this sort of shutdown is a temporary situation, and sexual health will rebound to previous levels. Sometimes, however, the recovery takes longer, and the individual may note a new, diminished level of sexual health or a new problem with sexual function.

POSTDEPLOYMENT REINTEGRATION AND SEXUAL HEALTH

The sexual response cycle, the progression from desire through arousal and maintenance to climax, does not always work as hoped. Especially in periods when the body is challenged overall, sexual function may be imperfect or work only some of the time. One such period for service members is the "reintegration" period after returning from combat deployment and rejoining civilian or garrison life. While this might seem like a joyous time—the warrior returns from combat, alive and ready to move on with life—it can be very stressful. The warrior must unlearn attitudes and behaviors that were adaptive in theater but interfere with daily activities stateside. He or she must renegotiate role expectations with family members and friends and find or retake employment or other gainful activities. During this period, sexual function may become a challenge for many men and women.

Reestablishing intimate relationships during the reintegration period might seem like an especially fun activity, but after an absence of many months, it can take established partners some effort to get back into the groove. Sometimes, things are good for a few months, and then the reunion honeymoon is over. The challenges that were at first swept under the rug in the interest of maintaining a happy, welcome-home feeling rise up and demand to be addressed. Sometimes, things are a challenge from the moment the service members walk off the plane.

Connie was an army reservist who deployed to the Gulf War from 1990 to 1991 at the age of 30. When she returned home, her husband, Doug, met her at the base with a hug and a crying two-year-old. He was fed up with the challenging experience of working and managing the house alone for 10 months with their three children under seven years old. Connie immediately jumped back in and tried to resume her previous roles and responsibilities, including returning to her old job as nurse but now on the night shift. This was too much, and she was soon completely burned out and depressed. The "honeymoon" of coming home lasted less than 12 hours for her. She and her husband found no time for themselves, and they engaged in almost no sexual activity or even physical intimacy. Doug was especially disturbed by this change in their pattern; Connie just seemed to be avoiding any physical contact with him.

Unrealistic expectations and new difficulty communicating with each other can complicate the reintroduction. Working together toward success at this point may be critical to avoid perpetuating or exaggerating the problems with sexual relations and broader relationship issues moving forward. Many veterans can reflect on their first few months home after deployment and realize how their behavior and reactions within their relationship led to subsequent events and outcomes. For some, this includes negative outcomes, including separation, divorce, and exclusion from their family.

Steve remembered how when he got back from Vietnam, he took up again with his girlfriend, and they were married. It lasted six months. In retrospect, Steve realized he had anger issues, and after a couple similar episodes, one night he got so upset about his inability to keep an erection during sex that he started yelling at his wife and blaming her for his difficulty, calling her hateful things. She went back to her parents' home that night and filed for divorce within a week.

The focus of optimizing sexual health for 18- to 30-year-old service members and veterans is generally on exploring opportunities, identifying a partner, establishing a family (if desired), and solidifying one's sexuality and thereby defining the parameters of sexual health for you. This is a period in which mistakes can be made and corrected but also the period in which patterns and preferences are established and can lead to suboptimal sexual health and even sexual dysfunction if they are unhealthy or too rigid.

SEXUAL HEALTH AND MILITARY SERVICE IN MIDLIFE

Not everyone in the military is young. In recent years, there have been approximately 1.3 million active duty service members in any given year, most of whom serve three to four years and then move back to the civilian world completely or transition into the National Guard or reserves. Relatively few service members remain on active duty and continue their service to retirement (usually after 20 years of service). By their thirties and forties, those who remain on active duty usually take on leadership roles and are fully integrated into a military base or unit and immersed in military culture. They may have to relocate frequently for new duty assignments and to maintain progress in their military career. Retirement for many comes when they're in their forties and fifties.

Since 2001, there have been around 850,000 members of the National Guard and reserve components of the U.S. military per year, and on average, compared to active duty personnel, reserve and National Guard personnel are older, more likely to be in a stable partnership, raising families, and employed in civilian jobs.[2] Reservists and National Guard members generally live integrated within a community separate from a military base. They also tend to stay in their communities. These differences between active duty service members and National Guard personnel and reservists can have an impact on an individual's sexual health, especially through the social setting, cultural norms and expectations, and challenges to the relationship.

CHANGING SEXUAL HEALTH AND PRIORITIES IN MIDLIFE

Sexual health evolves, and a new phase is identifiable in most individuals in their thirties and early forties. Rather than seeking new partners, most men and women at this stage of life are trying to maintain and strengthen their existing relationships, often in the context of rearing children. Many are in the peak years of productivity in their employment and careers, trying to solidify financial health and stability. Even with everything going as planned, sexual health may be a lower priority for many. The challenges of rearing children, maintaining a home, striving with one or two careers in the household, and fulfilling other social and civic responsibilities are daunting and often take priority over sexual health issues or even regular sexual activity. This is also true of service members.

After his first failed marriage immediately after his return from Vietnam, Steve took some time to sort out his life before he remarried at the age of 27. He had started a new job after dropping out of college and felt like things were going to work out for him. He wanted his new bride to stay home once they had kids. They eventually had three kids, and his wife did stay home. After the birth of their third child, it seemed that sexual activity for them became a twice-a-year event, but neither Steve nor his wife worried about the infrequency of their sexual activity too much.

The midlife stage is marked by a noticeable reduction in sexual activity. Higher-brain functions, both conscious and unconscious, offer a counterweight to impulses or urges that might have been pursued at an earlier age. Whether these urges are triggered by seeing an attractive person walking by or perceiving flirtatious behavior in an acquaintance, the risks and costs of engaging in sexual activity to the existing stable partnership, in compromising social status, or just forgoing other activities within the limited time available may be too great to act on the desire. As more of these urges get suppressed, the connections in the brain encouraging such urges become less potent, cementing the new pattern of behavior.

SEXUAL HEALTH CHALLENGES IN MIDLIFE

Sometimes, desire is sparked in response to someone other than a spouse or regular partner. Most people resist these urges and forgo sexual activity outside an established relationship. Infidelity does occur, however, and can have dramatic consequences. Why does it occur? There are probably more reasons than there are extrarelationship affairs. Each situation has its own unique set of circumstances. Three general conditions may contribute to the likelihood of an affair: (1) dissatisfaction with the established relationship, (2) the opportunity to meet potential partners, or (3) the opportunity to engage in extrarelationship sexual activity.

When Tom finally was able to talk to Lisa about why she had the affair with this guy named Ruben, she elaborated on how it was a mistake, how she was feeling lonely, and how it just seemed to happen. It wasn't a premeditated encounter or the result of her searching for someone; she met him, and he was there. Tom acknowledged how his absence during deployment made it difficult for her to stay true to him, especially since they were new to the area when he deployed and they didn't really have a strong network of family or friends available. He was still angry that she didn't resist the temptation but could kind of understand how it happened.

While deployment can create a separation between partners, the issue of infidelity is not unique to the military or veteran population. In fact, there is probably little difference between military personnel and civilians in terms of the opportunity to meet new potential partners or engage in extrapartnership sexual activity. For those male service members recognized by peers as "family men," the military culture likely exerts additional pressure to maintain the established relationship for the sake of the family, similar to general U.S. society. In contrast, there may also be military cultural influences perpetuating bachelorhood or a persistent quest for new conquests in a subset of men into later years.

Mark, the 37-year-old navy "lifer," was married to Mary, who lived in California with their children. During his 19 years of service in the navy and numerous tours in the Pacific, he knew exactly where to go to meet women in all the major ports. Sometimes, he found a willing partner, usually at a bar. Sometimes, he resorted to paying for sexual favors at brothels. With select friends, he boasted of never having been caught in a legal issue and never catching a sexually transmitted disease. Many younger sailors would follow Mark to the bars and egg him on when it looked like he was going to "get lucky." As he got older and began to think about his retirement, Mark wondered how it would be to settle down with his wife and kids.

At any life stage, the health of a relationship is more than the sum of its parts, but this may be an especially important factor in midlife relationships. It is the combination of the individuals' health and wellness as well as the intersection of these independent parts. For example, two partners can be very happy with their jobs, health, hobbies, and even family situation, but if their interests diverge, there may not be enough holding them together to make each of them say "I'm happy with my relationship." Other times, there is resentment between partners about roles or responsibilities, perhaps perceived as limitations on the ambitions of one partner, holding him or her back from realizing his or her full potential.

The importance of optimizing the sexual health of the relationship, like that of its overall health, may vary among relationships. Some couples find sexual activity very important to their relationship while others do not. Within the relationship, the partners may have divergent impressions of their shared sexual health. The frequency, type, and perceived quality of sexual activity can all be sources of discrepant perceptions. Discordance in the perception of sexual health can become problematic. One or even both partners may be unhappy with the situation yet uncertain how to improve it. This potentially could contribute to the dissatisfied partners seeking opportunities with others.

When Tom noticed that he couldn't achieve orgasm when engaging in intercourse with Lisa, he reduced his requests for sex activity with her. This abrupt change in his behavior worried Lisa. She wondered what had changed in him, as she enjoyed their pattern of sexual activity. She thought perhaps he had found someone else and worried about his having an affair. She also wondered if he found her less desirable for some reason. After they talked about his not having an orgasm, they went on the Internet and discovered that it was likely a side effect of the medication he started a month earlier. Both felt relieved and scheduled a visit to discuss it with Tom's doctor.

Given the impact of military and combat experience on sexual health as discussed in chapter 4, it is possible to trace how these influences might contribute to midlife challenges in maintaining sexual health in a relationship. The same issues of sex-based roles and expectations may creep into the relationship, potentially resulting in significant differences in preferences between partners. Persistent or recurring problems with sexual function may compromise or alter sexual activity in terms of frequency, type, or quality.

Steve, the Vietnam veteran in his sixties, had recurrent issues with his expectations for sex-based roles throughout his life. Recall that when Steve lost his job in his thirties, his second wife went back to being a teacher's aide. His continued insistence that she take care of the house and kids led to increasing resentment until she left him and took the kids.

Even after three failed marriages, Steve still thought that he could dictate the roles within the relationship. Perhaps his fourth wife would be happy with the role he assigned her, but more likely Steve's inability to communicate and negotiate with his previous partners would yet again compromise the health of the relationship and the sexual health of both of them.

Prior to her deployment, Connie enjoyed sexual relations with her husband, Doug. Connie experienced an especially rocky reintegration, and she and her husband were very preoccupied with their three children, work, and everything else. Connie also just wasn't feeling quite right since her deployment. Given their increasingly hectic schedules as the kids got older, it was pretty easy for her to find reasons to not engage in sexual activity with her husband throughout their thirties. Doug, in particular, was not happy with this, and eventually he sat her down to talk about why they weren't physically intimate anymore.

Sexual health and function in midlife is characterized by less frequent sexual activity for both physiological and social reasons. To optimize sexual health and function in this phase of life, you should regularly assess, for yourself and with your partner, your satisfaction and challenges. Through honest self-appraisal and open communication with the people who matter to your sexual health and function, you can better establish personal priorities and shared priorities for regularity of sexual activity, types of sexual activity, and innovations and new ideas to stimulate and maintain interest.

SEXUAL HEALTH IN OLDER VETERANS

Veterans of the Gulf War and Vietnam War will recognize that their interest in and level of sexual activity has continued to decline with age. It may be a more common occurrence that they can't become sexually aroused enough to engage in satisfactory sexual activity. They may not climax the same way they did when they were younger. Women experience menopause and dramatic changes in their hormonal balance that introduce new bodily symptoms, such as hot flashes, vaginal dryness, and changes in hair pattern. These can directly and indirectly affect sexual desire, arousal, maintenance, and climax. Men experience gradual declines in testosterone and related changes in body hair pattern, lean muscle mass, and percentage of body fat. These are the changes that happen with aging in any person.[3]

The role of military or combat experience in changes to the sexual response becomes less clear in older veterans. It is clouded by the accumulation of other, chronic health problems, such as cardiovascular disease, hypertension, and cancers. For those who remain in the military into later life (after age 50), obviously the social and other environmental factors encountered as part of their military service can affect their sexual health. For those who separate from the military earlier in life, the intervening years of exposure to civilian life's social and environmental factors exert substantial influence on sexual health and may obscure residual impact of all but the most striking contributions from military service. There are no data that truly tease out whether there are any independent effects of military experiences on sexual health or function in later years.

That said, once again, the effects of the military may theoretically contribute to the senescence of sexual health. As noted in chapter 3, combat is hazardous not only to short-term health and survival but also to long-term health. By their fifties and sixties, many veterans look back and conclude that their productivity and quality of life have been compromised and continue to be compromised by the damage incurred in military service. Most body systems come with some redundancy or reserve capacity. Damage to these systems early in life may not be detected immediately and may not be problematic except when the system is under stress. Unfortunately, this reserve also naturally erodes away over time with continued challenges to the body system, and eventually the available capacity doesn't meet the demands of everyday living.

For some veterans, the challenges experienced during deployment to or training in harsh conditions sapped their system reserves beyond usual for their age. That could mean that even with the same or less stress over their remaining life, their reserve will be used up earlier. For example, chronic musculoskeletal problems from the physical demands or trauma during deployment can produce nagging pain that can worsen over time or develop into arthritis and degenerative joint problems, especially without proper rehabilitative interventions and attention to avoid additional damage. Similarly, progressive hearing loss to the point of being unable to participate in a conversation in a public place may be accelerated in former military personnel. Many military personnel experience prolonged exposure to the noise of military equipment or cumulative damage from especially noisy or oto-traumatic events.

This phenomenon of reduced redundant capacity, although not rigorously documented with epidemiological research, would lead more quickly to the point of insufficient system capacity. Diseases related to the underlying deficiency would become apparent earlier and more noticeably in former military personnel. From available research, it appears that deployed military personnel may have lower overall health than nondeployed peers and civilians and have higher rates of chronic conditions, such as diabetes, hypertension, obesity, sleep apnea, and heart disease.[4]

The general accelerated decline in health in veterans degrades sexual health, too. As noted in chapter 4, some of the chronic conditions can contribute to or are associated with sexual dysfunction, especially in the arousal, maintenance, and climax phases. For these reasons, some veterans may experience earlier and perhaps more marked decline in sexual health as they age.

Laurie entered menopause at the age of 46. She suffered "the usual," as she said, hot flashes, thinning scalp hair, and dryness of her vagina. She tried some soy-based herbal remedies to help with the hot flashes, changed her hairstyle, and got some estrogen cream from her gynecologist after a discussion about her menopause in general and the vaginal dryness in particular. Her cohort of women former military officers were going through similar changes, and it made it easier to talk about with them since they had shared so many other experiences together in the military.

Steve was in bad health at the age of 62. He was obese and had high blood pressure, emphysema, diabetes, and sleep apnea. His interest in sex was greatly diminished, and his ability to get and maintain an erection was always in doubt even when he was interested. Steve couldn't help but wonder how much his military experience—and perhaps even his Agent Orange exposure—contributed to his current state. On the other hand, a number of guys from his unit had already died of things like cancer and heart attacks, and Steve was grateful to be alive. Since he was getting remarried to a young woman from the Philippines, he hoped she would stick with him and help him through his old age. He wasn't looking for much sexual attention from her, just some companionship and caregiving.

For Steve, it was probably too late, but for many recent combat veterans, it is critical that they invest in health promotion by eating healthy, exercising, and avoiding harmful activities and substances. It is easier to lose the excess weight in your twenties than in your forties, and by doing so and keeping the pounds off, you can actually delay the onset of the killers: heart disease, diabetes, and cancer.

Even if you're diagnosed with some of the chronic diseases like high blood pressure, high cholesterol, and diabetes, it's not too late. Making the lifestyle modifications to improve fitness and lose weight can still make a tremendous difference on mortality and sexual function. Taking medications as prescribed can also improve your chances of feeling better and living longer.

Once you decide to make the investment in your health and well-being, discuss your challenges, goals, and plan with your health care provider. When you implement your plan, keep a log and follow up regularly with your provider to make sure you stay on track and adjust the plan as needed. This sort of focused attention can promote health and function, both overall and in the realm of sexual health, for many years.

SUMMARY

Sexual health is important at all ages of the human life, although what optimal sexual health means varies dramatically over the life span. Even in shorter time periods, sexual health and function can wax and wane with changes in the many contributory factors. The trajectory of military service interacts with the trajectory of sexual health in interesting and important ways over the life span of an individual.

7

AM I NORMAL?

WHAT IS "NORMAL"?

"Normal" is a difficult concept to define, especially without resorting to a stereotyped view. While discussing stereotypes, this book tries to explore the origins and implications of those stereotypes related to sexual health and not blindly perpetuate them. There is no simple definition of "normal" for any particular aspect of sexual health or function. Instead, there is a range of what's acceptable, which varies depending on the setting and context. Ideas of what is "abnormal" sexual health may be more generally accepted, but defining abnormal is fraught with challenges, too. This chapter explores the range of sexual health by highlighting what most people would consider less-than-optimal sexual health and providing appropriate context.

Sexual health has been defined as a state of complete physical, mental, and social well-being related to sexuality and not merely the absence of disease or infirmity. Just like overall health, a person's sexual health is fluid, usually fluctuating within a normal range for that person and occasionally taking a more dramatic turn up or down. It represents a balance, a homeostasis, reflecting all of the inputs related to the sexual health of an individual. As some inputs change, the balance is shifted, and the individual must adapt to a new level of sexual health, perhaps adjusting an attitude, perhaps seeking additional input of some other factor, perhaps changing behaviors.

Both Joe and Megan had to adapt to new circumstances after Joe's traumatic brain injury (TBI). As he recovered, they realized they were not returning to their previous baseline frequency of engaging in sexual relations three or four times a week. Joe was far less interested in sexual activity, could hardly get an erection, couldn't maintain it long enough for his wife's satisfaction, and was very dissatisfied with the experience. Luckily, they had a strong relationship and were able to talk about the challenges and agreed to work together and try different positions, sex toys, and other ideas to optimize their sexual health. Although it wasn't the same as before, they were happy with the results of their experiments.

Tom and Lisa had to adjust to several changes in their circumstances. First, they had to change their habits after realizing that sometimes Tom would act out his nightmares and unknowingly threaten Lisa in his sleep. Sleeping in separate beds became the new normal for them, even after engaging in intimate sexual activity. Then, when Tom discovered the notes indicating Lisa's infidelity, it took a period of several months before they were able to repair the damage to their relationship and regain a large measure of the trust that was lost. For a while, it seemed like every time they disagreed about something, Tom would find a way to raise Lisa's infidelity. Lisa wouldn't see the relevance to the situation at hand, and the issue would escalate. Eventually, they worked with a counselor, going to four sessions together to find a way to resolve their differences and agreeing to put the affair behind them. Finally, just when things seemed to be getting back to "normal," Tom started the medication to help with his symptoms of posttraumatic stress disorder (PTSD), and they soon realized he wasn't able to climax. After their initial concerns about possible explanations, they realized it was likely the medication and worked with Tom's doctor to address this medication side effect. Over the course of three years, their relationship went through several ups and downs but held together, and at this point they were quite satisfied again.

In these vignettes, each of these challenges to the individual's sexual health was intertwined with their relationship. The impact of each challenge had broader repercussions and meaning, and their reactions to these challenges were critical to moving forward. "Normal" for each couple looked very different after deployment compared to before.

How do we assess our sexual health? We can look holistically at our behaviors, beliefs, and attitudes about sexual activity and the relationships involved. Examining the physical, mental, and social consequences of these behaviors, beliefs, and attitudes can provide an indication of our sexual health. There is no simple checklist to diagnose a problem given the complexity of sexual health.

A good starting point is your own sexuality. Sexuality is a personal construct reflecting one's ability to experience and respond to erotic thoughts and activities. It becomes part of the individual's identity—part of the answer to "who am I?" As an individual develops and matures, sexuality may shift quite dramatically until sometime in the late teens and twenties, when most individuals' sexuality settles into something more consistent. Some people have a very rigid concept of their sexuality, while others may be more flexible. The degree of comfort with diverse and new erotic thoughts and exposures is reflective of one's sexuality. Taking the time to think about basic questions like "how important is sexual activity to me?" or "what are my preferences in an intimate partner?" can help an individual gain great insight into this important part of him- or herself. If you know yourself and know what you want, you're far more likely to achieve success.

Another effective self-assessment is by following the components of the sexual response cycle. Thinking systematically about your body's sexual response can provide significant insights into potential problem areas. The human sexual response cycle includes sexual desire, arousal, maintenance, and climax. The complete absence of any of these components of sexual function is usually considered abnormal and reflects a significant alteration in the underlying body structures or processes. Short of complete absence, the range of experiences in each component, as well as what an individual would consider normal, varies considerably. Perceived problems in any phase of the sexual response cycle may be related to body structure or function, the setting or environment, social influences, mood or stress, or a combination of these and other factors. The problem may be present for a brief time or may persist over a lifetime.

RANGE OF NORMAL

Baseline Desire for Sexual Activity

Some people want a lot of sexual activity, and others want none. Some are quick to recognize a potential partner, and others are resistant to engaging in conversation or other interactions that might lead to a new relationship or sexual activity. There are so many factors that contribute to an individual's baseline level of desire that it would be impossible to be comprehensive in discussing them.

Looking back at an extended period of time, perhaps 6 to 12 months, and asking two questions can help identify a problem with your level of baseline desire. First, is your interest or attention to sexuality or sexual activity getting in the way of other things you want or need to accomplish? Do others imply that you might be overactive sexually? Second, are you unhappy because of your lack of interest in or opportunities for exploring your sexuality and engaging in sexual activity? If you are in a consistent relationship, asking your partner to answer these questions about you might be informative as well.

If the answer to the first question is yes, you may need to think about modifying your behaviors related to desire. It might be more challenging to suppress the feelings, actually dialing down the thermostat, so to speak. Exerting better control over the translation of those thoughts and feelings into words and actions is perhaps easier to accomplish and could be even more important to improving overall sexual health. Toning down the sexual content of your conversations, thinking about your body language, considering the activities pushed to the side by frequent sexual activity, and thinking about the motivation behind the overactivity may all be important actions to take.

Jonah described himself as a "raging hormone" when he first came back from deployment at the age of 22. He hadn't had sex in nine months and was thinking about it the whole trip home. When he got back to Pendleton, he headed straight to the strip clubs and spent three months chasing every girl he could. His friends hardly saw him, and even on leave to visit his parents, he was always talking about getting back to California, where the action was.

As discussed in earlier chapters, many other factors can affect expression of baseline desire. Peer groups can exert pressure to think or act certain ways, and substance use[1] can affect decision making about sexual matters in an unhealthy way.

One night, while Jack and his buddy were off base for a night, Jack's date was very drunk. Not knowing where she lived, Jack brought her back to the hotel with them. Jack's buddy encouraged him to have sex with her despite her drunken state. At the time, Jack was a little buzzed himself and decided that's why she went out with him in the first place, and she wasn't saying no. The next morning, the girl woke up crying and vomited several times. She called a friend to get a ride home and rebuffed Jack's efforts to be nice to her. Jack's friend was laughing, but Jack didn't feel good about the situation at all. For better or worse, he was being deployed in the next couple of weeks, and he just tried to put the episode to the back of his mind.

Clarissa hadn't gone out for a long time and was so excited about going to a party with her friend. Unfortunately, the next day, after having sex with the guy at the party with everyone in the next room, she felt embarrassed. That was not normal for her, and she wished she hadn't consumed so much alcohol, which clearly clouded her judgment. After the episode, she was left with several concerns about possible pregnancy or sexually transmitted disease and had to figure out how to get back to her normal.

If you're unhappy with your sexuality or level of sexual activity, solutions can be more challenging, especially for those focused on strictly defined sexual activity, whether by religious organizations, law, or perceived cultural norms. For example, just because your religion prohibits premarital sexual activity and masturbation doesn't mean your body doesn't experience the desires and arousal felt by people who don't belong to that religion and don't perceive the same importance of those restrictions. Rather than following their passion, some people believe their sexual desire must be channeled, delayed, or even denied to conform to cultural expectations.

Rhonda knew even when she entered the Marine Corps that she was more interested sexually in women than men. She did not admit to this and even dated men occasionally. After completing eight years in the Marine Corps, Rhonda was tired of denying herself a partnership she was truly interested in, but she didn't want to break the rules and didn't want to risk being caught. Despite glowing recommendations, she decided not to re-up her commitment and left the military altogether.

Others would like to enhance their sexual health but are unsure how to do so or are unable to determine why they aren't more interested. When this happens, it might be a good idea to consult a therapist, counselor, or a primary care or family physician. Seeking out help can be hard at first, but taking that step can result in the resolving of issues that may be holding you back.

After finally opening up to her sister, Maria sought treatment for PTSD and depression—a result of sexual assault experienced while she was serving. She was prescribed a medication and started individual therapy with a psychologist. As she started to feel better, she became a little more interested in her sexuality again and would find herself starting to think about an attractive friend and wondering if he might be interested in her. She wanted to begin dating again but still held back because of her fear of having to disclose her sexual trauma. Maria wasn't sure how to handle this issue.

Joe and Megan sought additional help with his low libido and difficulty with arousal and maintenance. They talked to Joe's primary care physician, who suggested blood tests to look at Joe's hormone levels. His free testosterone level was slightly low for his age, and they discussed low-dose supplementation with testosterone gel to see if this would increase his libido and his ability to maintain an erection. The doctor warned them that this might not fix the problem and could have side effects. They all agreed to try it for a few months and monitor what happened.[2]

SEXUAL RESPONSE CYCLE

Desire

The sexual response cycle begins with the noticeable increase in desire for physical intimacy focused on a particular individual at a certain time. Morphing from a vague, general level of consciousness about sexual interest, this desire phase of the response cycle represents a heightened awareness of interest and can incorporate a plan of action and imagined experiences.

So what can go wrong at this phase? Sometimes, memories can disrupt the transition into the sexual response cycle. Previous sexual trauma, for example, might inhibit one's ability to get into the mood for intimate sexual activity.

When Maria first came back from deployment and tried to reconnect with her boyfriend, every time they started getting intimate, she could not keep the memory of her sergeant from her mind. His face would appear to her so vividly that it felt to her like he was in the room with her. It repulsed her and made it impossible to continue making out with her boyfriend. It made all physical intimacy abhorrent to her.

Previous nontraumatic experience can also come to mind and interfere with initiation of the response. A persistent history of difficulty with sexual encounters can contribute to an attitude of "why even bother to try" and inhibit the full development of desire, short-circuiting the response.

Prior to her deployment, Connie enjoyed sexual relations with her husband. After returning from the Gulf, though, the few times she and her husband tried to engage in intimate physical contact, she was just too tired. She would try to go through with it, for his sake, but entry was always uncomfortable. Pretty soon, she would avoid almost all physical contact with him to discourage the possibility of intercourse.

Julio's use of alcohol, such as drinking before dates and drinking at bedtime to promote sleep, inhibited his ability to get and maintain an erection. When he was making out, he would realize he wasn't getting hard enough, and eventually he got to the point where he wouldn't even try to date. He kind of knew that alcohol could give him "limp dick," but he was convinced he couldn't succeed on a date without drinking. The cycle was one that was difficult for him to break, but eventually he started going to his primary care doctor, who recommended he seek treatment for his PTSD and alcohol abuse. Julio agreed to try it.

About two years after his back surgery, Jack experienced a recurrence of back pain and increased his use of an anti-inflammatory and opioid pain medication to manage this pain. He and his wife continued to engage in sexual activity, but Jack's interest began to flag, and the frequency was steadily decreasing. He just wasn't in the mood, and it seemed to be getting harder to get aroused. This change in pattern was not his idea of normal for himself—he was only 26 years old—and his wife was not happy with the situation at all. He realized he wasn't handling well this change in his health or its impact on his sexual health and function. He scheduled an appointment to discuss his pain with his primary care provider.

Another example of abnormal desire is a pervasive and constant attitude of boredom and the need for something new and different every time. Many people remember a particular sexual experience as the best and that nothing compares to it. Others maybe have so many sexual experiences that it becomes somewhat routine. These perceptions can make new opportunities appear less attractive or stimulating, limiting the desire to engage and proceed.

Jonah had numerous partners and sexual encounters before and during his service in the Marine Corps. It got to the point where he was generally uninterested in having sex with the same woman twice because he felt he knew what he was going to get. Sex with someone new, in contrast, provided some thrill of the unknown, and he was more interested. When on a second or third date with a woman, Jonah would sometimes end it quickly and before the expectation for sexual activity became too obvious. He would make an excuse and head home alone because he just wasn't interested in a repeat experience with many of his dates. He tried to not worry about this pattern, but he couldn't help but wonder if this was normal or if there was something wrong with him.

Arousal

Arousal often proceeds seamlessly from desire. The external genitals start to become fuller, leading to an erection in a man, and the woman starts to feel the lubrication of her vagina and vulva. The heart rate increases, and breathing becomes more shallow and rapid. These responses can be blocked by numerous factors, many of them similar to problems encountered in the desire phase. For example, anger, anxiety, and stress can "kill the mood" and cause couples to abort sexual activity in the arousal phase.

Unlike desire, which happens mostly in the brain, the mechanics of becoming aroused require more of the intricate processes throughout the body to align and work together to lead to the engorgement of the genitals and other changes. Arousal requires signals to be transmitted from the brain to the rest of the body by nerves and hormones in the blood. This makes the arousal phase more vulnerable to disruption by such things as alcohol, other substance misuse, medication side effects, and structural problems.

Juan had a severe TBI, other hormonal abnormalities, and a profound deficit in testosterone. Not only was he not interested in sexual activity, but he rarely experienced the background erections that men often experience as early morning erections. He began to experience these more frequently and began to actually think more about sexual activity once he started on his low-dose testosterone replacement.

Jack finally went to his primary care physician and asked about his lack of desire and difficulty with arousal. They discussed how it wasn't definitely the cause but that chronic use of opioid pain medications can suppress testosterone and contribute to these symptoms. The doctor suggested that Jack taper off the hydrocodone and use other techniques to manage his back pain. Then he would be able to see if the opioid pain medicines were helping overall or if they might be contributing to some of the things that were bothering him, such as decreased interest in sexual activity and difficulty with arousal.

Women also have difficulty with arousal, including insufficient engorgement of the vulva and a lack of lubrication. Some of the same medicines that contribute to erectile dysfunction in men can have equivalent effects on arousal in women. Inadequate arousal can make vaginal intercourse uncomfortable or even painful. Using lubricants can facilitate penetration, if that's desired, and may improve the quality of the arousal experience for the woman.

Maintenance

The maintenance phase is also prone to difficulties. A balancing act, maintenance requires not only the transmission of signals from the brain to the rest of the body but also feedback from the body to the brain to keep things going while not pushing so far that climax becomes inevitable. For this reason, all the factors that can impede desire and arousal are also potential pitfalls for the maintenance phase.

Climax

Climax is the culmination of arousal and the point at which the maintenance phase successfully ends. It is almost a "yes-or-no" experience.

While there is a qualitative nature to climax, many experience climax as either achieving orgasm or not. Let's start by discussing why you might not climax.

Humans cannot climax without the preceding phases of the sexual response. If the processes fail before climax, you won't get there. That means that anything that interferes with the desire, arousal, or maintenance phases of the sexual response cycle will keep you from experiencing climax. There are times when a person might get stuck in the maintenance phase and not be able to reach climax despite ongoing efforts. You just can't quite get to that tipping point of release. Sometimes, this can reflect a less-than-optimal stimulation experience. The situation may feel good but not quite good enough. It could also represent an experience in which some of the sensations feel good but some do not, and the suboptimal totality of the experience keeps you from reaching climax.

Joe and Megan had found some very creative and effective solutions to Joe's difficulty with maintaining an erection. Together they had explored various positions and oral sex, even trying sex toys, such as a vibrator, when Joe's penis wasn't cooperating. They realized, however, that these substitutes were not always as good as what they remembered from before Joe's TBI. Megan often would be feeling really good, and Joe would be into it, too, but then Megan wouldn't quite get to climax. "What can I say?" Joe told his primary care doctor when they were following up on his sexual health issues. "She just likes my dick."

Sometimes, medications can impede progression to climax. Selective serotonin reuptake inhibitors (SSRIs) are prescribed for PTSD and depression and are known to block climax, as might other antiseizure medicines and even opioid pain medications.[3] Alcohol and stimulants can also interfere with the nerves that control climax, preventing it from happening.[4]

After Tom started his SSRI to help manage his PTSD symptoms, he realized he could still get and maintain his erection, but no matter what he tried, he could not climax. He first realized this when he and Lisa were having intercourse one night. Everything felt really good, but he reached a point where he was just tired; his wife was climaxing, and he wasn't even close. He faked his own climax and wondered what had happened. He tried masturbating the next day in the shower and had the same problem—he just wasn't reaching climax. After that, he mentioned it to Lisa, who pointed out that he had started his SSRI about a month earlier. They looked up the side effects on the Internet and saw that SSRIs can delay or inhibit orgasm. That day, Tom scheduled an appointment with his primary care doctor to talk about the side effects and alternatives.

A related side effect of SSRIs (and potentially other medications as well) is retrograde ejaculation. As mentioned several times, the balance of controls around arousal, maintenance, and climax are finely balanced. Sometimes, when the balance is off in a man, the semen is propelled backward into the urinary bladder instead of out through the penis. This doesn't usually cause any harm, as the semen is eventually voided with urine, but it would make it difficult to conceive a child. It might also leave the participants in the sexual activity wondering where the semen went.

Another problem sometimes encountered in men is premature ejaculation or climax. It is often associated with youth and relative inexperience with sexual activity but can also affect older and more experienced men. This is also related to the balance of all the factors controlling climax. Once again, there is a range of normal for the time between arousal and climax for men, but if the man or his partner perceives that the time is too short, it can be considered premature.

Edward, the young man with the moderate TBI and the difficulty getting around, met Jacquie, an attractive physical therapy assistant trainee who did a rotation with one of his therapists. After she had moved on to a new rotation, she sent Edward an e-mail, and things moved forward from there. Eventually, they were on a date, and things were going very well. One thing led to another—they were kissing, and way before they were ready, Edward climaxed and ejaculated. Although somewhat disappointed, both laughed about how long it had been since he was with a woman and decided to call it a night and schedule another date for the following weekend.

NORMAL IN INTIMATE RELATIONSHIPS

If proposing a range of normal for an individual's sexual response is challenging, it is even more difficult to define the range of normal for a couple. An individual can know what to expect when masturbating, creating an opportunity to understand one's own body and sexual response. During masturbation, you have control over most of the factors that determine success—a pleasurable sexual response culminating in orgasm and climax. Your brain sets things off with desire set up in your own imagination and triggers arousal. You control the stimulation to the body and therefore the feedback to the brain during maintenance, and you also have more control over the timing of climax.

When engaged in sexual activity with a partner, you give up some of this control and rely much more on the partner for the physical, emotional, and behavioral stimulation to intensify and maintain desire and promote complete arousal, maintenance, and climax. All the while, your partner is requiring the same of you. There's no wonder that sexual activity with a partner is often less than optimal for one or both parties.

A few basic concepts can be relevant to determining whether there are any opportunities to improve a sexual function with a regular intimate partner. First, look back at the sexual response for both partners in the shared sexual encounters over a time period. Consider all the interactions, even those in which sexual activity stopped before arousal. Compare and contrast them and consider other sexual activities outside the relationship, past or present, and examine the same characteristics of those experiences. This might include masturbation and perhaps encounters with other partners. Second, examine the context of the relationship: living situation, opportunities for sexual activity of varying types, competing demands, and external social pressures or expectations. Finally, explore how the sexual activities, frequency, and the life situations interrelate. Where do the partners perceive things similarly? Differently? What contributes to the well-being of both partners? To the well-being of one or the other? Some couples might be very happy having sex once a month, while others may be happy with once a week. This sort of systematic assessment can produce a shared understanding between partners that can help establish a range of expectations for sexual activity and contribute to the partners' mutual sexual health.

STRUCTURAL CHALLENGES THAT REDEFINE SEXUAL HEALTH

For service members and veterans with other structural deficits of the body, sexual health is affected by the mechanics of engaging in sexual activities. For example, missing arms, scars, burns, and facial disfigurement can make it hard to find a partner or may require unusual approaches to promote their or their partners' arousal.

Ted, missing part of his left leg and left arm, never seemed to have a hard time getting a date. On the other hand, moving the dinner or conversation to the bedroom was more difficult. Women didn't seem to know what to expect from him in bed. It took him some time and energy to figure out what he was comfortable with and how to optimize his chances of exciting his partner as well. He had to coach his partners on what he could and couldn't do given his missing arm and leg.

Clarissa had concerns about her body's functions as well. Who would want a woman in a motorized wheelchair? What would she be able to do and feel? How could she retain a sense of control that was critical to her? She also knew that she was incontinent of urine and wasn't sure how this would affect her participation in sexual activity or her partner's perception of the experience. The night she drank too much and engaged in sexual activity at the party, the alcohol erased these concerns, at least until after the fact. She decided that she would need to do more planning and perhaps some experimentation by herself through masturbation to see what her body did during sexual activity. She also thought about mentioning it to the female nurse at her physical rehabilitation center to see what ideas she had.[5]

David's minimally responsive state after his catastrophic TBI presented Susan with even more profound challenges. She was committed to David and held out hope that he might recover more fully, but there seemed to be little chance of their engaging in any sort of consensual sexual contact. She worked with her minister to figure out how she could maintain her sexual health while ensuring her dedication to David.

Jonah sometimes used a condom and sometimes did not. After a one-night stand on Saturday, he woke up on Tuesday with an itchy, burning sensation at the tip of his penis, and then a creamy white liquid started flowing out. He called his primary care doctor's office, had to schedule a visit for the next day, and spent a lot of time and money taking care of his sexually transmitted disease and being tested for other possible infections. His doctor told him to not engage in sexual activity for at least a week to allow the antibiotics to take effect and minimize the chance of becoming reinfected or infecting others.

During their sporadic attempts at intercourse over the years since she returned from the Gulf War, Connie experienced increasing discomfort and even pain when her husband tried to insert his penis into her vagina. It felt like her vagina was being stretched or ripped, and she couldn't do anything to relax it. She felt bad about this and eventually went to her gynecologist to discuss possible solutions. Her gynecologist reassured her that she had seen women with this problem before and that they would work out a strategy to improve the situation.

After menopause, Laurie noticed that she had some spotty bleeding from her vagina again. She immediately went to the gynecologist and soon was told that she had some precancerous cells on her Pap smear and would need a hysterectomy. Laurie was grateful that they caught the problem before it became more serious, but it took her many months to recover from the procedure. She did not engage in vaginal intercourse for almost a year and was not sure if she returned to her baseline interest and satisfaction even at that point.

Steve's primary care provider performed his annual screening for prostate cancer when Steve was 64 years old and found a suspicious level of prostate-specific antigen. Steve was reluctant to have the biopsy, the next step in the work-up to see if cancer was present, but finally agreed to go through with it. Luckily, the biopsy did not confirm prostate cancer, but Steve found the procedure, which involved inserting a device into his rectum and jabbing a probe into the prostate, so unpleasant that he declined all further screening for prostate cancer. He did not want to undergo that procedure again.

SOCIAL AND INTERPERSONAL FACTORS ALTERING SEXUAL HEALTH

There are a number of other issues that can impact sexual health of an individual and sexual relations between partners. This book cannot address all of them or delve too deeply into all the different facets of these issues, but the more common ones are introduced to highlight areas that might need more evaluation.

Violence

Sexual health is a state of complete physical, mental, and social well-being related to sexuality. A corollary of this definition is that any sexual behaviors should contribute to the well-being of the involved individuals and not injure or diminish their health. Unfortunately, this is not universally honored, and emotional, verbal, or physical abuse in the context of sexual relations occurs all too frequently. Sometimes, even otherwise loving individuals can cross the line and inflict damage on a partner; there should always be some consideration of a pattern or intention, but when someone gets hurt in a sexual activity or in an intimate relationship, it should be further evaluated by a counselor or, in more extreme examples, by law enforcement or medical personnel.

Some individuals express a desire to engage in activities that might cause bodily harm to themselves or to their partners in the context of a sexual encounter. Willful attempts to cause harm or requesting others to cause you harm is not consistent with the World Health Organization's definition of sexual health. Experts in sexual health can be engaged to further discuss these desires with an expert (see chapter 8).

Knowing the Rules

Some behaviors are regulated by laws or organizational rules, affecting how they are perceived, whether as normal, abnormal, or in some gray zone. Some are banned entirely, and others are restricted in various ways. Examples of these activities include prostitution (receiving or giving money or goods in exchange for sexual activity), adultery, sodomy (e.g., oral or anal intercourse), possession and viewing of pornography, and homosexual activity.[6] Different countries, states, and even local governments have varying rules on these issues, making it essential to understand the rules depending on where you are.

The diversity of the restrictions about these activities highlights differences in opinion about these activities. Some people believe that some or all of these sexual activities are abnormal, unacceptable behaviors, and others think that they're perfectly acceptable. Geographic variations in the rules may reflect different dominant beliefs in particular regions. The differences in restrictions may also reflect differences in tolerance for public and private acknowledgment of these activities. In some places, the laws may be active but rarely or only selectively enforced.

Military service members are expected to behave according to the rules set forth in the Uniform Code of Military Justice, as discussed in chapter 2. In addition to several articles related explicitly to sexual behavior and activities, there is the catchall chapter of the code making it criminal to engage in "conduct unbecoming." The possibility of prosecuting crimes related to sexuality under this clause is one way in which military leaders reinforce cultural sexual norms among service members. The lack of explicit criteria allows for subjective application of this clause based on the particular circumstances of the episode or the prevailing norms of the environment or unit.

As discussed in earlier chapters, substance abuse, especially binging on alcohol, is commonly associated with sexual activity and poor choices about sexual activity. Intoxication is generally not an acceptable excuse for illegal behaviors, and this is true of crimes of a sexual nature as well.

Finally, the age of consent for sexual activity also varies from place to place. Every culture and legal jurisdiction has an age below which sexual activity is not considered appropriate. The age of consent often differs by the sex and relative age of the participants. For example, in the same state, the age of consent for men may be 14 years, but the age of consent for women might be 16 years. It may depend on if the young man is older than the young woman or vice versa. Finally, there may be different rules if the two are the same age or within a certain age of each other. For younger military service members, some of whom join with a deferral at age 17 years, these rules matter, and knowing them can be critical to making good decisions.

Too Much of a Good Thing

Occasionally, men and women engage in sexual activities too often or in inappropriate settings. When the amount of activity or choice of venue interferes with other activities, such as work, school, or home life responsibilities, it could be considered a problem. Sometimes, this exuberance of activity is temporary and can be easily reined in, but sometimes it is a sign of a more serious problem, such as substance abuse or the mania associated with bipolar disorder. If you get a feeling your sexual behavior is out of control or someone you love is behaving like this, it's important to seek help from a mental health professional.

Risky Behaviors

Sexual activity is not without risk. By engaging in sexual activity with a partner, you are exposing yourself to his or her body, his or her desires, and his or her actions while simultaneously giving yourself over to your own sensations. This can be a wonderful experience, but it can also result in undesired consequences in the form of physical or emotional damage, infectious diseases, or unwanted pregnancy. There are many things one can do to minimize the risk of these occurring. Most people choose to engage in some sexual activity that's commensurate with their tolerance for risk.

First, monogamy with someone you know is usually safer than engaging in sexual activity with multiple partners or people you don't know very well. Having an established relationship with a sexual partner provides many advantages: you may know some of that person's sexual experiences, where he or she lives, what he or she does, and how to contact him or her again later if necessary. In an established monogamous relationship, you likely (although not always) have made a commitment to exclusivity, whether formally recognized, as in a marriage, or less formally. After being together for a period of time, knowledge of preferences and quirks grows, and you adjust to each other's needs and desires, perhaps improving the sexual experiences and reducing the risk of unintentional discomfort or harm. You are also likely more attuned to new things in your partner and can ask about any new issues that might come up.

Learning all these things about more than one partner can be challenging; it takes time and effort. Managing the disappointment and other effects if clandestine sexual activities are discovered could be catastrophic for the primary relationship and have a serious detrimental impact on the sexual health and overall health of both partners. Even in the context of an open relationship, one in which both partners explicitly agree to tolerate sexual activity outside the relationship, balancing

competing demands can be taxing and result in jealousy and degradation of the quality of life.

Engaging in anonymous or near-anonymous sexual activities raises
the risk of unhealthy consequences, including sexually transmitted diseases and violence. Without the established social connection, the consequences of mistreating a partner or not disclosing relevant sexual
history can seem less important: "I'm never going to see this person
again." This attitude is not consistent with the World Health Organization's definition of sexual health and healthy sexual relationships. Of
course, not all casual encounters are negative experiences, but by stick-
ing to more established relationships, the risk of harm and unintended
consequences is reduced.

Second, consider using barrier protection. Condoms are an important option in sexual activity, especially early in relationships or with
new partners. Condoms are most protective with penetrative sexual
activity, when the penis enters the vagina, anus, or mouth. Condoms
limit exposure to semen, which can carry infectious agents like human
immunodeficiency virus (HIV) and bacterial causes of sexually transmitted diseases. It can also reduce the penis's exposure to these same
agents from vaginal secretions and the minute quantities of blood
present during vaginal and anal intercourse. Condoms really do reduce
the rate of transmission of sexually transmitted diseases if used properly
and consistently. Even with the occasional failure, regularly using condoms can promote sexual health for both partners.

Condoms also are effective at reducing the rate of pregnancy—
though they are not foolproof. A condom is a visible, verifiable indication of protection from unwanted pregnancy. A woman may know she's
taking her oral contraceptive pills and feel that her risk of becoming
pregnant is therefore minimal. Her male partner, on the other hand,
has no way of knowing whether she took the pills regularly, whether she
might be on another medicine that interferes with their effectiveness,
or whether she even might be intentionally misleading him. Condoms
are a very helpful way to increase the certainty of contraception. Using
condoms allows the male partner to take ownership of the decision to
not create a pregnancy. Pregnancy can create additional decisions and
downstream challenges, including, potentially, parenthood and responsibility for a child and family. For men having sex with women, if chil-

dren are not part of the plan with this woman, it is best to use a condom.

A final way to minimize risks in sexual activity is through moderation of alcohol use and avoiding illicit substances. As mentioned several times throughout this book, alcohol and other substances can impair decision making. This can lead to unhealthy choices related to sexual activity and some of the consequences alluded to in this chapter. Just as with overall health, maintaining sexual health requires a degree of self-management, and alcohol and other substance abuse can dramatically interfere with self-control and determination.

SUMMARY

As we discussed above, there are many factors to consider when assessing one's sexual health and intimate relationships. By focusing on a sense of normal that applies to an individual and his or her relationships, a thoughtful self-assessment can result in improved insight into problem areas and challenges that can be addressed, as discussed in chapter 8.

8

LET'S TALK ABOUT SEX

Pop songs are full of good advice, right? They mention sex as though it were *that* easy to talk about, that casual. But the truth is that it's very difficult to talk about sex in any serious way, and to discuss sexual health issues is even more difficult for most people. Yet communication is probably the most important factor in optimizing sexual health, especially in the context of a committed relationship. Communication is the bidirectional sharing of ideas and understanding. It is not only words but also the nonverbal cues of body language and actions, tone, and active listening. Sometimes, the spoken words conflict with the actions and body language, and the sharing of ideas and understanding is muddled.[1]

The need to communicate is a universal human need, and military personnel, current and former, practice communicating daily. Practice is perhaps the key word in that sentence; we all can get better, and every day we encounter new situations requiring new ways of communicating. For those who suffer with sexual health concerns or experience sexual dysfunction, there is hope. By building on existing communication skills and networks, these individuals can take the first steps toward a solution and experience hope.

When thinking about who to talk to and where to get help, a stepwise approach is probably most effective. Some issues can be resolved through conversations with your partner (if you have one). Talking openly about thoughts, concerns, perceived failings, and new desires can often create intimacy that may help in the bedroom. Other concerns may benefit from discussions with a broader network of supportive friends and family, many of whom may have experienced difficulties themselves or know where to find help. Some issues may take more expertise and require the involvement of trained experts with various training, knowledge, and experience. This chapter describes the many options for accessing help for the diverse problems related to the sexual health of service members and veterans.

WHO CAN I TALK TO?

Your Partner

Sexual health can be one of the most challenging topics to discuss in a relationship. As discussed previously, sexuality is a core feature of our identities, and discussing this openly with a partner can be like exposing your inner secrets. For many, sexual activity with their partners is also a key defining aspect of the relationship; it's what makes it special and different from the relationships with other friends and family. Implying less than total satisfaction with the shared intimacy can be fraught with concern. How will he or she perceive the feedback? Will he or she get angry and withdraw from me? Will he or she take it seriously? Will we be able to get back on track? There is real potential for some conflict and emotional pain in these conversations.

On the other hand, by having an open discussion about sexual health concerns, there is the potential for an even stronger relationship and better sexual health for both partners. For most established couples, there is only one regular partner, and this person knows the other's sexual preferences better than anyone else. Your partner may be able to share some observations or insights you haven't even considered. Also, think about the alternative of not engaging in the discussion; would you be happy enough if things continued the way they are now? Play it out a little bit. What would you do if your intimate encounters didn't address your concern? Would you get bored? Would you withdraw and choose not to engage? What would that do to your relationship? If you don't address your concerns, things might even get worse. A listing of the pros and cons of raising your concerns should be considered prior to having the talk. However, sometimes avoiding the topic can ignite other problems within the relationship when a problem is evident and not being discussed.

Joe and Megan had been through a lot with his injury and then the shift in their shared sexual health. They were not always happy with the situation but realized they needed to talk about things. They were not always happy with the conversations, either, but overall they respected each other, loved each other, and wanted to work things out. Their relationship was definitely stronger even with the new normal of their sexual health.

Preparation for the talk may be appropriate, too. Think through your concerns and hone your points so you can communicate the issues more precisely. Think about how to frame them. Try to be as positive as possible and avoid placing blame. Talk about behaviors or actions rather than attributing these to the person. For example, say "I'm disappointed when you do this" instead of "I'm disappointed in you." Can you be constructive in your feedback? Can you offer potential solutions? Instead of just "Your penis hurts me when you enter me," consider adding something like "We should try having your penis enter me from a different angle."

Engage in mutual, creative problem solving in these conversations. Think of how you might have contributed to the situation and be prepared to accept responsibility. Volunteer your role to the issue and offer to hear how you could do better. If it's a question of frequency of sexual activity, perhaps you could look back and talk about how more or less might have been possible or appreciated. If it's an issue of opportunities passed over, was your partner even aware of your attempt? Make sure you've accounted for contextual issues as well as your direct concerns.

Timing can be critical. You may not want to bring about your dissatisfaction with a lack of orgasm right after sexual activity that ended with your husband being upset about losing his erection and having to call it quits for the night. That would not be sensitive to his feelings and could add to his frustration. On the other hand, using a supportive approach may make this the best time to bring up a desire to work on sexual relations together and share some ideas of how to enjoy the intimacy without his erection. Taking him by the hand and showing him how to satisfy you without an erection could be an effective, appreciated response.

If your wife always seems to refuse your advances, ask her what you can do differently. When is the best time to ask her about sexual activity? When is it a bad time? What words can you use? What if she tells you something you don't want to hear? How will you react?

Connie and Doug had a lot of issues in their relationship. Doug was growing increasingly frustrated with their lack of sexual activity. Their kids were older, and they had more time to spend with each other, but Connie was clearly avoiding physical intimacy with Doug. Eventually, he brought it up directly with Connie, and she confided her lack of sensation and discomfort with vaginal intercourse. Seeing that the problem for her involved pain and discomfort, Doug was much more understanding of her distance, did not want to see her in pain, and wanted her to find help. They decided that she should discuss this with her gynecologist to see what was going on.

Sometimes, it helps to have the conversation about sexual health and dysfunction with your partner in the presence of a counselor who can facilitate the discussion and maintain a safe and healthy setting for the conversation. Counselors who offer this service to couples may follow various approaches, depending on their training and experience. There is more discussion of the types of counselors below.[2]

Trusted Friends and Family

Sometimes, you may not be ready to talk directly to your partner. Or perhaps you're having issues with sexual function and you're not in a stable relationship. It can be helpful to identify a trusted friend or family member to talk to. Of course, not everyone needs to know about your sexual health. Sexuality is an important but deeply personal attribute. People generally choose to share or disclose information about their sexuality to the people closest to themselves. Sometimes, being more open can complicate matters.

An example of a sexual health issue that people are usually comfortable discussing with friends and family is a feeling of strong desire for someone that is not reciprocated. Similarly, sharing how you're trying to fend off the expressions of interest of an uninvited suitor is a fairly acceptable topic of conversation among friends and family. These topics are also at the center of many stories in books and movies, and most adults are pretty comfortable navigating these waters. Younger people with less experience in relationships may feel less confident in their abilities to handle these issues. Given the importance of dating and social groups in the teens and twenties, many young people may feel that certain decisions could have important implications on their social life and sexual health. Many service members are in this stage of life, and negotiating relationships and the sexual activity sometimes associated with them is a common topic of conversation. Somewhat personal and sensitive but usually not "high stakes," discussing the challenges of interpersonal relationships with friends and family can result in new perspectives and ideas for how to handle the situations. There may be benefits to gathering a wide variety of input.

Other topics, such as difficulty with arousal, maintenance, or climax, are typically considered much more personal and sensitive and are not generally shared very widely with friends and family. This is perhaps due to the perceived stigma of experiencing these challenges and the possibility of a negative impact if the information were shared more widely. Certainly, in discussions with military personnel, humor at the expense of those experiencing sexual dysfunction is commonly reported. This is especially true of younger service members. The teasing could be good natured or more of a derogatory nature. Regardless, most individuals would discuss issues like erectile dysfunction or lack of vaginal lubrication only with a few close friends.

Eric made it through boot camp and was sent to his first duty station in rural Louisiana. He fell in with a good group of men and women. He felt comfortable sharing his concerns with them, and when he realized he was interested in dating a woman from town, he was able to read up on the rules and talk it through with some of his peers. When he finally approached the young lady at the mall, he was devastated to realize she was already engaged but recovered gracefully. It took him a while, but eventually he could laugh about it with his friends.

Finally, some topics are so uncomfortable, such as sexual violence or abuse, that individuals will go to great lengths to cover them up. Concerns about the legal and associated social and financial implications may also contribute to the silence about these issues. This suppression can perpetuate the problem, however, and result in additional harm to the victims as well as delay effective interventions to help the perpetrator. Confiding abuse or violence, however, is usually the first step toward healing. Whether to a friend, family member, or trained professional, such information is usually met with concern, care, and assistance. When issues of a more serious nature are shared, it is important to direct the individual to the right experts or authorities to help assist with the situation.

Rhonda separated from the Marine Corps and moved near her elderly mother. She began to explore the dating scene and met some nice women on a gay swim team. Rhonda swam in high school but not much since. Rhonda tried going to the practices once or twice a week and enjoyed the camaraderie and regular physical exercise. She soon began to date one of the women on the team.

The Internet

The Internet is full of accurate information and good advice and also full of much inaccurate information and wrong advice. Using the Internet to learn about sexual health and dysfunction is an especially common practice because there is so much information available and because it's relatively anonymous. With a stigmatized and taboo subject like sexual health, having access to the Internet seemingly provides a safe means of learning more and identifying a path forward.

There are a few principles that can maximize your chance of finding accurate information and good advice on the Internet. First, as a primary source of information, avoid websites that try to sell products to enhance sexual health or treat sexual dysfunction. Many of these sites are selling ineffective, untested, and unregulated products, and it is difficult to accurately assess which ones are reputable and which are not.

Second, there are websites that are recognizable as credible sources of information (see the Resources section of this book). Many are official government websites that have content related to sexual health and health care, including the Department of Defense, the Veterans Administration, the Centers for Disease Control and Prevention, the Department of Health and Human Services, and the National Institutes of Health. State and local governments may also have some relevant and credible information. Large academic medical centers and health care delivery systems may also have useful and reliable information, although some of these institutions may also be trying to build up their patient base and provide specific services through these websites.

Third, there are other reliable sources of information, such as consumer health sites and patient advocacy sites. Reading through the Web content can often indicate how robust and experienced the sponsoring entities are; look for when the website was last updated, the quality of the writing, the type of links to other sites, and viewers' feedback and comments.

Finally, corroborate anything you find on the Internet with other sources, including other websites and your own knowledge. Share the information with friends and family, as appropriate, to get others' impressions of its validity and usefulness. Discuss your findings with your health care providers. Make sure you bring a printout of the material to the appointment or can pull up the website when asked so that he or she can see exactly what you were reading. This approach can result in a really efficient way to get on the same page with useful information and ideas about solutions. If it's difficult for you to find the words to say to a professional, printing material and handing it to your doctor may help bridge that gap.

PROFESSIONALS WHO CAN HELP

Sometimes, it's important to talk to a professional. Whom you first reach out to is partly a matter of convenience but should also take into account the type of problem you're dealing with and, it is hoped, the informed opinions of others who have worked with that professional. Medical providers, such as physicians, nurse practitioners, or physician assistants, may provide assistance, especially if the issue involved has a physical component. For active duty service members, the unit corpsman or medic may be a convenient first stop with straightforward questions or advice on where to go for help with more complex problems. Some problems have relatively easy fixes, such as vaginal dryness in a postmenopausal woman. Erectile dysfunction is now treatable in many cases with medications.

While a medical condition may exist, it may be a good idea to find out why such dysfunction is happening and how to get at the root causes. For these issues, a mental health professional is recommended. In some cases, a sex therapist may be the way to go, but most psychological and psychiatric professionals have some training in this area and can be of assistance as well. The following sections describe the types of professionals who are trained to help with sexual health issues and sexual dysfunction.

Counselors and Sex Therapists

Sometimes, it helps to discuss sexual health with an expert. While many different professions offer help with sexual health issues, there are certified sex therapists who are professionals who are credentialed by the American Association of Sexuality Educators, Counselors, and Therapists (AASECT). These experts have graduate degrees (often in psychology or social work), complete course work and mentored training in sexual health and function, and agree to abide by the AASECT code of ethical conduct.

Certified sex therapists are trained to follow the P-LI-SS-IT model of assessing and treating sexual health concerns. First, the therapist establishes a comfortable, supportive environment with the client by receiving *permission* (P) to question and explore concerns. Then the therapist provides *limited information* (LI) to fill in any important gaps in the client's knowledge. *Specific suggestions* (SS) require more detailed inquiry by the therapist about the sexual history of the client and probing for the issues, context, and perceptions that contribute to the concerns. Finally, the therapist can initiate *intensive therapy* (IT) to address the priority issues identified together with the client. This systematic approach to sexual health can be very effective and can ensure a more comprehensive assessment.[3]

Certified sex therapists can work with an individual or with a couple. Depending on the problem, the therapist may be able to use his or her other professional training and certification to address it more comprehensively or may need to partner with other health care providers. For example, the sex therapist may recognize depression as a major contributing factor but not be able to prescribe an antidepressant to treat the depression directly. A referral to a psychiatrist or a primary care doctor may be warranted.

Mark's wife, Mary, saw it coming. When Mark retired from the navy, she was ready to help him reintegrate with the family life on a full-time basis, but she insisted on working with a counselor in couples therapy. Mark saw how important this was going to be and felt grateful that

Mary had taken the initiative to get this set up for them. It wasn't easy, but working with the counselor helped them talk through their grudges, prejudices, and anxieties. It also helped them coparent their teenagers, who were beginning to experience challenges in their sexual health around this time as well.

Military Paraprofessionals (Corpsmen and Medics)

For many service members, the corpsman or medic affiliated with their unit is their "doc." This term of endearment and respect is usually well deserved and earned through loyal service in challenging, shared experiences. Asking doc for recommendations on how to proceed with appropriate medical evaluation and treatment for a possible sexually transmitted disease or getting access to condoms is perfectly appropriate. It is often easier and more comfortable for some service members, especially enlisted, to approach the medic than to approach an active duty physician or nurse practitioner. Those personnel are officers and likely the ones who told you to "wrap it" with a condom before heading off for rest and relaxation.

Looking for more detailed information or more sophisticated evaluation and treatment will likely require the involvement of a more highly trained health care professional. Once again, the corpsman or medic can facilitate that handoff and ensure that you get to the right person. The best docs know their limits and will advocate fiercely for their men and women to get the right care.

Jonah called his corpsman that Tuesday morning he woke up with the burning and drip from his penis. His corpsman sympathized with him, but after letting Jonah vent a bit about how frustrated he felt with his situation, he told him what to expect and directed him to sick call for the right evaluation and treatment.

Julio was hitting bottom in his new city. He reached out to his former corpsman via Facebook and told him about how bad he was feeling. The corpsman called another buddy of theirs who lived near Julio and escorted him to the nearby Veterans Administration (VA) facility. Julio was not admitted to the hospital but was closely followed by a counselor and the suicide prevention coordinator for several months. He was able to cut down on his alcohol use significantly and enrolled in vocational rehabilitation through the VA. His former corpsman continued to call him every couple of days, and he started socializing with the buddy who lived nearby and his wife and kids. With his symptoms of posttraumatic stress disorder (PTSD) better controlled, improved sleep, and a pathway to employment in place, Julio began to feel more hopeful about realizing his goals of a real job and a real girlfriend.

Clergy and Chaplains

For some people, sexual health is deeply enmeshed in their spiritual beliefs and their involvement in organized religion. For these individuals, some sexual health issues can present additional concerns, such as divine reprobation or even a belief in eternal damnation or denied access to paradise. For example, many religions take issue with or condemn premarital sexual activity, the use of contraception, sodomy, homosexuality, and adultery. Recognizing and trying to resolve discrepancies between the physiological urges, the ever-present temptations of day-to-day life in modern America, and the beliefs required based on the teachings and expectations of an organized religion can be terrifying, paralyzing, and demoralizing for some people. This is a personal challenge at the intersection of faith and sexuality that generally requires time, contemplation, and gathering and synthesizing a variety of perspectives.

Sometimes, approaching a leader in your religious organization can be an appropriate and helpful approach to certain sexual health concerns. In an ideal world, these religious counselors would also have specific training in sexual health or other clinical qualifications, but that is often not the case. Religious leaders may have the authority to speak to the faith aspect of sexual health concerns but may not have all the answers.

The military employs chaplains of various religious denominations and orders. For active duty service members, these personnel may be accessible and provide assistance of both a spiritual and a practical nature without engaging the formal military health care system or chain of command. Most commonly, they offer a nondenominational spiritual guidance as opposed to faith-specific expertise. For those not ordained in the faith of the concerned individual, they can often also refer to a colleague of that faith.

Jonah struggled with his isolation while garrisoned with his unit and sought the counsel of the chaplain. He also struggled with his attitude toward women, his pattern of casual sex, and his subsequent lack of interest in sex after being a "raging hormone." He liked the calm approach of the reverend, even though Jonah was raised Roman Catholic himself. As he began to think about what might come after his military service, Jonah talked more and more to the reverend about going to seminary and pursuing the calling of minister. He didn't think he could handle the celibacy required to become a priest of the Catholic faith but was going to ponder the impact on his sexual health.

Health Care Providers

Seeking health care for a sexual health issue can be challenging. Many of today's clinicians were trained to diagnose and treat diseases and continue to take a biomedical approach to health concerns. This can mean that they deemphasize the mental and social factors, the context of the disease. Ever-shorter appointment slots with most providers add to the challenges of a more holistic approach, too. Unfortunately, sexual health concerns almost always engage mental and social factors as much as or even more than the biomedical considerations. The best sexual health care utilizes a biopsychosocial approach, looking at the context of the structural or functional defect in the body and addressing the situation holistically. Finding the best sexual health care can be a challenge.

Many physicians, psychologists, nurses, and physician assistants have little formal training and experience in sexual health concerns. Just like many others in U.S. society, many health care providers view sexuality and sexual function as taboo subjects and are uncomfortable bringing them up in a clinical encounter. Research shows that only about one-third of individuals with sexual health concerns reported that their doctor brought it up in their visit. In one survey, more than 50 percent of doctors felt uncomfortable conducting a sexual history. Very few doctors or clinics screen individuals for sexual dysfunction. Even when screening is conducted (often a single item on a checklist completed in the waiting room), responses indicating a problem may be ignored or postponed until other conditions and concerns are addressed. Finally, doctors may discuss sexual dysfunction but then not know what to recommend, what further evaluation to perform, or where to refer patients. They may reach for the treatment they know best and not consider alternatives.[4]

When Joe first started talking with his primary care doctor about his lack of desire, his doctor said, "I have exactly what you need," and wrote him a prescription for a PDE5 inhibitor. Joe thought, "I'm 26 years old, I shouldn't need that stuff," and didn't even fill the prescription.

Patients can help their providers do better by being more explicit about the importance of sexual health concerns if those concerns are the desired focus for the visit. It will help for the patient to prepare for the discussion. Write down the questions or concerns prior to the visit and bring the paper with you. Get input from your partner if he or she is aware of the issues and write down his or her questions, too. Bring your partner along to the appointment. Using proper terminology can be helpful to ensure clear communication between the provider and the patient and can minimize distraction and confusion from informal labels or slang. Emphasizing the impact of sexual health concerns on everyday life can help providers understand how important the concern is and may facilitate more complete evaluation.

Primary Care Providers

Primary care refers to health care that is accessible for first contact, nonemergent concerns. Ideally, it provides continuity and coordination of comprehensive care that is individualized for each patient. The health care industry in general is promoting universal access to primary care, using the term "medical home" to describe a team-based approach to coordinated, timely evaluation and management of health concerns. This is not a new concept, but the economics of the health care industry appear to be increasing the presence of this approach. In many parts of the United States, people are very accustomed to using a primary care provider who may then refer the patient to an appropriate specialist. In some parts, however, people still go directly to specialists, depending on the problem or symptom, and the medical home concept may require a shift in their health care utilization pattern. The Veterans Health Administration (VHA) and Department of Defense military treatment facilities emphasize a primary care–centric approach to health care in which every patient is assigned to the panel of a primary care provider.

Very soon, this will be the standard approach for all active duty service members and veterans who use the VHA.

In the absence of more generally available health care practitioners specialized in sexual health, primary care providers can be an excellent first place to go with questions about sexual health. Given the biomedical emphasis of medical training, sexual health concerns that intersect with concerns about other, nonsexual health problems or their treatments may provide an excellent starting point for the conversation. For more complex sexual health concerns, the primary care provider can make the necessary referrals to specialists to perform further evaluation and ongoing management.

Jack continued to have flare-ups of his back pain about three times a year. Sometimes, he required muscle relaxants and low-dose opioids for a few days around the flare-up to manage the pain. His primary care doctor carefully monitored his use of these medicines and encouraged appropriate physical activity to promote healing and strengthening of Jack's core muscles. Of course, when the pain was bad, Jack and his wife weren't sexually active, but Jack did notice that in between these episodes, he felt better and more interested in sex than when he took more of the pain pills than he was supposed to. That became an important reminder for him of why he should take only what his primary care doctor prescribed.

When Tom and Lisa discovered that Tom's inability to climax might be related to the selective serotonin reuptake inhibitor (SSRI) prescribed for his PTSD symptoms, Tom immediately called his primary care provider to report the problem and ask what to do about it. The doctor called him back and suggested that Tom start tapering off the SSRI and try a different kind of SSRI. He explained that there are several slightly different but equivalent kinds of SSRIs and that the new medication might not have the same side effects. He advised Tom to keep an eye on the issue with the new medicine and to schedule a visit in six weeks to discuss his PTSD symptoms and sexual function in more detail.

Steve became more dependent on his fourth wife, and the focus of his visits to his primary care provider was on his chronic medical conditions and the medicines they used to manage them. On one visit, Steve, out of the blue, asked if he could have the "little blue pill." Knowing exactly that he meant a PDE5 inhibitor, his provider asked him to tell him some more about the request. Steve acknowledged that while he often didn't feel in the mood, occasionally he did, and he would like to have some help getting aroused. The provider looked at his wife, who shrugged and said, "If that's what he wants." The provider reviewed Steve's medicines to ensure that there wouldn't be any negative interactions and, when convinced there weren't any obvious problems, wrote the prescription for Steve. The next visit, Steve reported he had tried the pill about three times with some success and was grateful for the opportunity to enjoy physical intimacy with his wife. She smiled, slightly embarrassed, but put her hand on Steve's arm.

Mental Health Providers

For veterans and service members, PTSD, major depressive disorder, and substance abuse are among the most common mental health conditions. In fact, almost 50 percent of veterans who use the VHA have one or more mental health condition, and even among veterans who don't use the VHA, mental health conditions are a common health problem.[5] As discussed in previous chapters, mental health and its treatment can have significant direct and indirect effects on sexual health. For these reasons, a mental health provider can be an excellent resource for additional information about sexual health concerns for a veteran or service member.

Mental health providers are a varied bunch. There are psychiatrists, who are trained as physicians (with MD or DO degrees), who tend to focus on prescribing and managing medications for patients with the most serious mental illness. Psychologists receive a different training (resulting in PhD or PsyD degrees) that focuses on psychosocial function and counseling techniques to address problems. There are other professionals, such as psychiatric nurses and social workers, who received different types of training but also focus on psychosocial concerns and offer counseling services. Finally, a big proportion of mental health care is provided by primary care providers, especially for mild to moderate mental health conditions. Primary care providers are likely to manage mild depression or PTSD, especially in the VHA or military health care system. For more serious problems or advanced medication management, however, mental health providers are more appropriate.

Mental health providers may have the expertise, time, and inclination to assist with the evaluation and management of sexual health concerns or may deemphasize them. This depends largely on the training, experience, and setting of the mental health provider's practice and, of course, the client's needs and preferences. While most mental health providers are able to recognize sexual health issues and refer to specialists in this area, they may be no more or less likely to screen for or address sexual health issues than a primary care provider. In the context of individual counseling, if the client identifies sexual health issues as an area of concern, it is more likely that the mental health provider will address the issues explicitly, but even in that situation, treating the primary mental health concern, such as PTSD or depression, according to an evidence-based therapy may be the priority.

Maria continued to struggle as her interest in dating increased because of her concern that she would have to disclose her history of sexual trauma. She wasn't sure how it would go, but she decided to mention it to her regular mental health counselor. She worked with her counselor both to address the trauma she experienced as a result of sexual assault and to figure out a plan for communicating with potential partners with which she was comfortable. She decided that after a few dates, she could start to tell a dating partner about her reluctance to rush into sexual activity and see how he responds before moving forward with more. Maria felt better just having a plan in place.

If the severity of the condition warrants the involvement of a mental health provider, especially a psychiatrist who is prescribing psychoactive medications, the prescriber is generally aware of the medication's side-effect profiles. Unfortunately, many of the most effective medications for treating the common mental health conditions of deployed veterans can cause or contribute to difficulties with the human sexual response.

MEDICATION MANAGEMENT STRATEGIES

As noted in chapters 4 and 7, there are many medications that are known to cause or contribute to sexual dysfunction. Given the high prevalence of mental health conditions and the known effects of SSRIs and other psychoactive medications on sexual health, these are especially important to recognize and be able to manage. There are other medicines that can contribute to sexual dysfunction. These include antiseizure medicines used for treating and preventing migraine headaches and other nerve pain, opioid pain medications, and blood pressure medications.

Regardless of who prescribes the medicines or the specific type of medication, there are a number of approaches to managing the suspected adverse medication effects on the sexual health of the patient. A conversation between the patient and the prescribing provider or the coordinating primary care provider is critical to determining the best approach to addressing sexual side effects. Prescribed medications should never be adjusted or stopped without consulting a health care professional. Doing so could result in serious health implications in some cases.[6]

The first approach to addressing a suspected medication side effect is to stop or discontinue the medication after discussion with the health care provider. Sometimes, patients are prescribed medications that may not really make that much of a difference to their quality of life or long-term survival. Stopping a medicine that isn't doing what it's supposed to but that is causing a new problem may seem like an obvious solution, but without comprehensive medication review, this can be missed. For some medicines, it is important to taper the dose of the medicine instead of just stopping it abruptly.

Similarly, for some problems, there are nonpharmacological treatment or management options. For depression and PTSD, for example, sometimes patients are initially given the option of a medication with or without counseling, though counseling is often recommended in conjunction with medications. If the medications cause undesirable effects, patients and their providers should reconsider the counseling option. Unfortunately, for many conditions, such as migraines, medications are just more effective, especially in the short term.

The second approach is to switch medications if an alternative is available. For SSRIs, there are many similar molecules that have similar positive effects on depression and PTSD symptoms and may work better or worse in any given individual. If one type of SSRI is effective for the mental health symptoms but causes delayed orgasm, trying another SSRI may maintain the desired benefit and remove the problematic side effect. Sometimes, switching medicines can mean switching to another class of medication altogether, such as changing from an SSRI to a serotonin-norepinephrine reuptake inhibitor to manage depression. There may be less certainty that the desired beneficial effects will continue to be present if the medication class must be changed.

Other types of medications have few or no similar alternatives. In this case, you can taper the medication dose down a bit to see if the benefit remains while the undesirable side effect improves. This can work well with medicines that have been used for a while and the side effect gradually developed after the benefit started.

Another approach is to try a medication holiday, taking a break from the medicine and restarting it after a few days. This should be attempted only after discussion with a health care professional. Sometimes, this can confirm that the medicine is actually causing the side effect, or the side effect may not come back. If the side effect recurs, the patient and the provider can create a schedule that allows for recurrent "medication holidays." In the case of erectile dysfunction associated with an SSRI, skipping a dose or two just before a weekend, for example, when the patient anticipates he might have an opportunity to engage in sexual activity may improve his chances of a satisfying experience. This approach works best with the shorter-acting medications but can mean that the benefit of the medicine is weakened as well.

Another consideration is to add a different medicine to counteract the side effect. PDE5 inhibitors are often prescribed to men with erectile dysfunction due to an adverse effect of a medication, such as a blood pressure medicine. There are not many other medicines that reverse adverse effects so precisely, however, and the use of multiple medications raises the chance of other side effects or a negative interaction between the medicines.

Finally, using a second medicine with similar or complementary action can sometimes allow for a lower dose of the offending medicine. This should reduce the side effect while maintaining the overall benefit, once again at the risk of introducing a new set of side effects or an interaction between the medicines.

A key to success is communication again, this time between the patient and the prescribing provider. It may be advisable to engage the regular partner as well to get a slightly different perspective on issues such as changes in desire, arousal, and satisfaction with sexual activity.

Medication changes should not be undertaken without discussing them with the prescribing provider first.

OTHER SPECIALISTS

Gynecologists

Gynecologists are physicians who specialize in women's health, especially in the surgical concerns of women's reproductive organs and genitals. They almost always receive simultaneous training in obstetrics to develop the knowledge and skills necessary to help a woman manage pregnancy and deliver babies. Some women get annual pelvic exams, breast evaluations, and Pap smears from a gynecologist, while others rely on a primary care provider for these services. For many women, the gynecologist may serve as their primary care provider as well, especially during years of peak sexual activity and reproduction.

Gynecologists are generally very knowledgeable about women's sexual health issues, especially related to structure and processes of the genitalia and reproductive organs. They frequently prescribe contraceptives including birth control pills, intrauterine devices, and cervical caps and perform surgical procedures such as tubal ligations (to prevent future pregnancies). The specialized knowledge and expertise of the gynecologist is especially important for problems related to the menstrual cycle, abnormal vaginal bleeding, vaginal infections and sexually transmitted diseases, and pain with sexual activity. Many gynecologists take a comprehensive (i.e., biopsychosocial), approach to women's health and routinely address breast health and psychosocial issues as well. Gynecologists may have less formal training about the psychological aspects of sexual health but are likely to gain proficiency with these concepts through practice. Most will know sources of other specialized help to refer patients in need.

At her follow-up visit with the gynecologist, Connie brought her husband, Doug, with her. They provided the gynecologist with an update on their attempts at sexual activity and discussed Connie's continued difficulty with vaginal intercourse. The gynecologist explained directly to Doug some of her ideas about what Connie was dealing with and offered some suggestions to him about how to help Connie overcome the discomfort. Hearing the information directly from the gynecologist was very helpful to Doug, and he was able to ask her a few questions that he had as well.

After her hysterectomy, Laurie continued to follow up with her gynecologist, who continued to counsel Laurie on postsurgical exercises she could do to strengthen her pelvic muscles and approaches to manage the discomfort she experienced after the procedure. Laurie continued to get her prescription for estrogen vaginal cream. They also explored the information from the Internet about herbal remedies that Laurie brought in to her appointments.

Urologists

Urologists are also physicians who train as surgeons focusing on the male genitals and reproductive organs and the kidneys. Most urologists do not provide primary care for men and instead focus on patients with urologic problems referred to them by primary care providers. For this reason, urologists tend to see men with significant problems, usually related to structural or functional problems of the penis, prostate, bladder, or kidney.

Urologists, like gynecologists, also do not necessarily receive much formal training in the psychosocial aspects of men's sexual health, but most accumulate the necessary knowledge through experience. Because many of the surgical procedures performed by urologists can result in sexual dysfunction, all urologists have some familiarity with treating sexual dysfunction in men. Some urologists subspecialize, however, and it is important to recognize the particular focus of a urologist prior to the visit. This can be done by calling his or her office and asking about areas of expertise.

Some urologists do specialize in sexual dysfunction in men, and these experts may be more likely than a general urologist or one who specializes in a different aspect of urology to offer a comprehensive approach to the assessment and management of sexual dysfunction. The urologists who specialize in sexual dysfunction are likely to offer a range of options, including prescriptions for PDE5 inhibitors, as well as other, less commonly used medicines for erectile dysfunction, education and prescriptions for penile injections for erectile dysfunction, medicines for premature ejaculation, surgical implants for erectile dysfunction, and others. Most urologists are most focused on the issues related to genital structure and function and may rely on professional colleagues to address the psychological and interpersonal issues related to sexual health and dysfunction.

Ted followed up with an urologist after having a scrotal ultrasound that confirmed that there was no obvious structural damage to his testicles or vas deferens. They decided to conduct a semen analysis to determine if Ted had a fertility issue. Ted had to go to a laboratory and masturbate into a cup in a private room to provide a fresh sample. Happily, the results of that test came back normal as well. Simultaneously, Ted was discussing his options for diagnosing and treating the possible recurrent leg infection. He and the infectious disease specialist opted to continue to suppress the possible smoldering infection with antibiotics likely to work against the bacteria. He resumed sexual activity with his girlfriend, and they began to discuss a possible wedding.

Endocrinologists

Endocrinologists are physicians who train in internal medicine and then go on to specialize in the hormone systems of the body. This expertise can be critical in the evaluation and management of some forms of sexual dysfunction in both men and women. Endocrinologists also subspecialize, with some developing deeper knowledge and expertise in the hormone systems of women or men or specializing in various hormonal subsystems, such as the thyroid, pancreas, or adrenal glands. Because of the complexity of the hormonal milieu and how several different hormonal subsystems interact, a general endocrinologist may be a good place to start after a primary care provider performs some baseline testing and identifies a possible hormonal abnormality.

If sexual health and dysfunction is the concern, it is important to work with an endocrinologist with good knowledge and experience in this area. If infertility is a particular concern, this type of consultant should be engaged to maximize the chances of success. As mentioned in chapter 4, hormone test results can be very difficult to interpret accurately, and an endocrinologist can often help make sense out of the findings and conduct additional evaluations. If a deficiency in a particular hormone is discovered, there may be a relatively straightforward solution in terms of supplementation with the missing hormone. Often, however, the relationship between abnormal hormone test results and a sexual health problem is less precisely understood, and the endocrinologist may recommend a trial of a supplement. Sometimes, a hormonal abnormality may be suspected but not confirmed, and the specialist may recommend a watch-and-wait approach to see if the problem resolves or becomes more readily apparent through repeat testing.

Juan continued on his low-dose testosterone supplementation but didn't increase the dose a second time. He started acting out in the group home with some frequency and would have to be reminded to masturbate in the privacy of his own room. He perceived enough benefit from this level of supplementation in terms of both his sexual health and his overall fitness and he and his team decided to maintain the dose where it was.

Joe and Megan realized that testosterone supplementation didn't really make a difference in Joe's libido or his sexual arousal. Rather than continue the supplementation for his minimally diminished testosterone level, Joe concentrated on eating healthy and exercising regularly. He lost some of his excess weight and began to feel more fit and even more interested in sex. He accepted the prescription for vardenafil to improve his erectile function. He and Megan enjoyed a renaissance in their shared sexual intimacy although still at a lower frequency than prior to Joe's deployment.

Physical Medicine and Rehabilitation Specialists (Physiatrists)

For many people with complex injuries and permanent structural defects, physiatrists and their teams of therapists are miracle workers. With their knowledge and experience, the rehabilitation team can not only offer treatments to improve structure and function but also help create compensatory solutions, such as mobility aids, prostheses, and environmental modifications. With time, these experts see a broad range of problems and gather the best solutions they see in their patients, who improve their own lives through trial and error. Even in the realm of sexual health and function, the rehabilitation team is likely to have creative options for even the most troubling and personal problems. They will also know which other experts to pull in to work on the team to help the veteran or service member with sexual health concerns related to residual damage from polytrauma.

For David, Susan remained at his side with the support of her family and the paid caregivers. The physical rehabilitation team conducted regular assessments of David in their home and made sure that the latest technologies were employed to ensure safe and thorough care for David. Susan would occasionally take a ladies' weekend away with her friends; this provided her with some respite from her caregiving responsibilities. She also invested a lot of her attention in their daughter and began to thoroughly enjoy the routine of caring for David. It gave her great satisfaction to ensure that his quality of life was optimal.

Clarissa scheduled an appointment with her physical rehabilitation nurse specifically to discuss her sexual health concerns and to find out how to have a gynecology exam. She was relieved to discuss her experience and her desire to learn more about her own body and its potential for sexual activity. She was not pregnant, and her gynecology exam was scheduled within the month. Clarissa had several new patient education materials to read about sexual health after spinal cord injury and felt more empowered than ever after her surgery.

Edward continued to live with his mom, Doris. He didn't have too many more dates with Jacquie, the physical therapist assistant, but the experience gave him more confidence, and his buddies started taking him out with them more often. He began to feel more hopeful about meeting a woman to marry, and Doris was so relieved to see her son finally getting to spend time with his friends.

SUMMARY

Sexual health is ever evolving, and individuals and couples strive to optimize their sexual health and functioning. When things aren't going well, a stepwise approach to sexual health concerns is the best, ideally starting by engaging your partner in the conversation. Unfortunately, the taboo of discussing sexual health issues is pervasive and may be observed in the discomfort of even highly trained professionals. Preparation, self-advocacy, and appropriate communication can lead to improved understanding and the additional support necessary to address sexual health concerns. Seeking professional help when a discussion with a partner does not help the problems at hand is a good starting point for addressing not only sexual health issues but also the underlying physical, emotional, and mental health problems that may be contributing to them.

RESOURCES FOR VETERANS WITH SEXUAL HEALTH CONCERNS

RESOURCES FOR INJURED VETERANS

U.S. Department of Veterans Affairs

The Veterans Administration (VA) offers the entire range of benefits and information for veterans and service members who will become veterans. This includes health care, disability and other benefits, education and training, and more.

On the Web: http://www.va.gov

U.S. Department of Veterans Affairs Office of Public Health

The VA Department of Public Health website offers a multitude of information and resources for veterans ranging from specific health conditions to military and environmental exposures.

On the Web: http://www.publichealth.va.gov

U.S. Department of Veterans Affairs Vet Center Program

Vet Centers offer a wide range of services to veterans and their families at 300 community-based Vet Center locations across the United States.

On the Web: http://www.vetcenter.va.gov

War Related Illness and Injury Study Center (WRIISC)

A part of the Veterans Health Administration under the Office of Public Health, the WRIISC is a national VA postdeployment health resource, focusing on the postdeployment health concerns of veterans and their unique health care needs. It develops and provides postdeployment health expertise to veterans and their health care providers through clinical programs, research, education, and risk communication.

On the Web: http://www.warrelatedillness.va.gov

Wounded Warrior Project (WWP)

WWP is dedicated to fostering a successful, well-adjusted generation of wounded service members. Their stated purpose is to raise awareness and enlist the public's aid for the needs of injured service members, to help injured service members aid and assist each other, and to provide unique direct programs and services to meet the needs of injured service members.

Offering programs in mind, body, economic empowerment, and engagement, they seek to apply a holistic view in educating, empowering, and supporting injured veterans.

On the Web: http://www.woundedwarriorproject.org
Wounded Warrior Project
1120 G Street NW, Suite 700
Washington, DC 20005
Telephone: 202-558-4302

ADVOCACY AND LEGAL RESOURCES

American Bar Association (ABA) Military Pro Bono Project

The ABA Military Pro Bono Project accepts case referrals from military attorneys on behalf of junior-enlisted, active duty military personnel and their families with civil legal problems and places these cases with pro bono attorneys where the legal assistance is needed. The project is also the platform for Operation Stand-By, through which military attorneys may seek attorney-to-attorney advice to further assist their service member clients.

On the Web: http://www.militaryprobono.org

Outserve-SLDN (Servicemembers Legal Defense Network)

Outserve-SLDN is an association offering free and direct legal assistance to actively serving lesbian, gay, bisexual, and transgender (LGBT) military personnel and veterans. They are a nonpartisan, nonprofit, legal services watchdog and policy organization dedicated to bringing about full LGBT equality to America's military and ending all forms of discrimination and harassment of military personnel on the basis of sexual orientation and gender identity.

On the Web: http://www.sldn.org

Free legal hotline: 1-800-534-7418

MILITARY SEXUAL TRAUMA INFORMATION AND RESOURCES

U.S. Department of Veterans Affairs: Mental Health and Military Sexual Trauma (MST) Resources

The VA offers information and resources regarding services related to MST on their website under the mental health subsection. You do not need to have a VA disability rating (be "service connected") to receive these services and may be able to receive services even if you are not eligible for other VA care. You do not need to have reported the incident(s) when they happened or have other documentation that they occurred.

On the Web: http://www.mentalhealth.va.gov/msthome.asp

U.S. Department of Veterans Affairs—Make The Connection: Shared Experiences and Support for Veterans

This website offers shared stories, information, and resources for veterans who have experienced military sexual trauma.

On the Web: http://maketheconnection.net/conditions/military-sexual-trauma?gclid=CJaC8pKv7b4CFSwS7Aodey0A2w

LGBT RESOURCES FOR VETERANS

American Military Partner Association (AMPA)

AMPA's website provides information, support, and resources for LGBT veterans and their partners.

On the Web: http://militarypartners.org/resources

Outserve-SLDN (Servicemembers Legal Defense Network)

Outserve-SLDN is an association offering free and direct legal assistance to actively serving LGBT military personnel and veterans. They are a nonpartisan, nonprofit, legal services watchdog and policy organization dedicated to bringing about full LGBT equality to America's military and ending all forms of discrimination and harassment of military personnel on the basis of sexual orientation and gender identity.

On the Web: http://www.sldn.org

Free legal hotline: 1-800-534-7418

SEXUAL HEALTH RESOURCES FOR VETERANS

American Association of Sexuality Educators, Counselors, and Therapists (AASECT)

AASECT provides a professional referral for those seeking licensed, professional sexuality educators, sex therapists, and counselors.

On the Web: http://www.aasect.org/referral-directory

American Urological Association Urology Care Foundation

The Urology Care Foundation website offers high-yield specific information related to sexual health, ranging from prostate cancer and erectile dysfunction to bladder infections. Also provided is a Web-based referral tool to locate board-certified urologists in your area.

On the Web: http://www.urologyhealth.org

SexHealthMatters: Sexual Medicine Society of North America

SexHealthMatters addresses fertility and sexual health issues for veterans, including a wide range of information ranging from in vitro fertilization to erectile dysfunction.

On the Web: http://www.sexhealthmatters.org/for-healthcare-provid ers/addressing-fertility-and-sex-health-issues-for-veterans

WOMEN VETERANS HEALTH RESOURCES

American Congress of Obstetricians and Gynecologists (ACOG)

Considered to be the leading experts in women's health issues, ACOG provides a patient website featuring a wealth of information relating to women's health

On the Web: http://www.acog.org/For_Patients

National Alliance on Mental Illness: Veterans Resources and Women Veteran–Specific Information

The Veterans Resources section of the National Alliance on Mental Illness website has some good resources for information on traumatic brain injury, posttraumatic stress disorder (PTSD), and mental health issues related to service. It also offers a section that focuses on women veteran's health issues.

On the Web: http://www.nami.org/Template.cfm?Section= Veterans_Resources&Template=/ContentManagement/ ContentDisplay.cfm&ContentID=53587&lstid=879

Veterans Information Helpline: 1-800-950-NAMI (6264)

Office on Women's Health, U.S. Department of Health and Human Services

The U.S. Department of Health and Human Services Office on Women's Health offers a helpful website focusing on mental health and issues relating to female veterans. It offers specific information as well as links to other online resources relating to the following:

- PTSD and women veterans
- Military sexual trauma and women veterans
- Intimate partner violence and women veterans

On the Web: http://womenshealth.gov/mental-health/veterans

VETERAN SERVICE ORGANIZATIONS: GENERAL INFORMATION

American Legion

Focusing on service to veterans, service members, and communities, the American Legion currently has about 2.4 million members in 14,000 posts worldwide.

On the Web: http://www.legion.org

Disabled American Veterans (DAV)

Another veteran advocacy and assistance organization is the DAV. Their mission is to fulfill the country's promises to its disabled veterans.

On the Web: http://www.dav.org

Iraq and Afghanistan Veterans of America (IAVA)

Supporting health, education, and employment as its priorities for the newest generation of veterans, IAVA strives to build an empowered generation of veterans who provide sustainable leadership for our country and their local communities.

On the Web: http://www.iava.org

Veterans of Foreign Wars (VFW)

The VFW serves veterans by advocating for them as a community voice and providing direct assistance in filing disability claims and accessing health and educational resources.

On the Web: https://www.vfw.org/Pages/Form.aspx?ekfrm=4294970683

NOTES

INTRODUCTION

1. For more about the epidemiology of sexual dysfunction in the United States, see Laumann et al. (1999) and Waite et al. (2009).

1. WHAT IS SEX?

1. "WHO Definition of Health," last amended April 7, 1948, http://www.who.int/about/definition/en/print.html.

2. The World Health Organization's International Classification of Functioning, Disability, and Health provides a common language and framework for describing health and functional status. See Kostanjsek (2011).

3. Various references are provided that provide more detail on the anatomy, physiology, and human development of sexual and reproductive organs and systems. See Moore et al. (2011), Netter (2014), and Silverthorn (2012).

4. See Masters and Johnson (1966) for the original discussion of the sexual response cycle.

2. MILITARY CONTEXT AND CULTURE

1. See recent published research on the prevalence and epidemiology of sexual health/dysfunction in veteran populations, such as Helmer et al. (2013) and Hosain et al. (2013b).

2. Further explanation and examples of military organizational hierarchy and culture can be found in Holmes-Eber (2014).

3. Established by the U.S. Congress, Uniform Code of Military Justice (UCMJ) (64 Stat. 109, 10 U.S.C. Chapter 47) is the foundation of military law in the United States.

4. The Manual for Courts-Martial (MCM) is the official guide to the conduct of courts-martial in the U.S. military. The MCM details and expands on the military law found in the UCMJ. See U.S. Department of Defense (2012).

5. Within the UCMJ, *Conduct Unbecoming* and *General Article* (UCMJ Articles 133 and 134) are frequently subject to a broad range of interpretations by commanders in order to discourage and/or punish specific behaviors among military personnel. Servicemembers Legal Defense Network (2011), 18.

6. In January 2013, Secretary of Defense Leon Panetta rescinded the policy excluding women from combat roles in the military (Roulo 2014).

7. "Don't ask, don't tell" (DADT) was the official U.S. policy governing service by gays and lesbians in the military instituted by the Clinton administration in February 1994. The policy prohibited military personnel from discriminating against or harassing closeted homosexual or bisexual service members or applicants while barring openly gay, lesbian, or bisexual persons from military service (Chu 2011).

8. President Barack Obama, Defense Secretary Leon Panetta, and Chairman of the Joint Chiefs of Staff Admiral Mike Mullen provided the certification required by the Act to Congress on July 22, 2011, to repeal DADT. Implementation of repeal was completed 60 days later so that DADT was no longer policy as of September 20, 2011. See Bumiller (2011).

9. See Markle et al. (2013) and Stahlman et al. (2014) for more about the epidemiology of sexually transmitted diseases.

3. EFFECTS OF COMBAT DEPLOYMENT ON HEALTH

1. For more details on the casualties experienced by U.S. troops in Iraq and Afghanistan, see Fischer (2014).

2. Because it is such an important and official validation of combat injuries received, the Purple Heart medal often acts as a force multiplier in recovery from trauma and PTSD in veterans. For explanation of Purple Heart criteria, see Recognize the Sacrifice (2014).

3. To further understand the rehabilitation process as well as outcomes from polytrauma and blast injuries, see Sayer et al. (2008, 2009).

4. See the U.S. Department of Veterans Affairs publications included in the bibliography for more details. Particularly useful is U.S. Department of Veterans Affairs (2014e). See also Gironda et al. (2009).

5. Sayer and colleagues' research illustrates the possible sequelae by veteran patients after traumatic brain injury. See Sayer (2012).

6. See Ramchand et al. (2010) and Schnurr et al. (2010) for additional discussion about PTSD after being deployed to combat.

7. More is being learned about PTSD, thanks to significant and relevant ongoing research. Some current and foundational literature includes Benedek (2010), Friedman et al. (1994), Frueh et al. (2001), and Tanielian and Jaycox (2008).

8. For more detailed information on depression and other psychiatric disorders, refer to Tampi et al. (2008) and Tanielian and Jaycox (2008).

9. See Seal et al. (2009) for more information about substance abuse diagnosis among veterans using the Veterans Health Administration as well as other mental health diagnoses in this population.

10. Because sleep disruption and dysfunction are common in veterans suffering from PTSD, there is a large body of research on sleep disorders in these populations as well. See Mustafa et al. (2005) and Nolan (1995).

11. The bibliography contains several sources that delve deeper into the health concerns of Gulf War veterans and their possible causes. Consider Gronseth (2005), Iowa Persian Gulf Study Group (1997), Ishøy et al. (2001), Ismail and Lewis (2006), and Lange (2011).

12. For more information about Agent Orange, Gulf War syndrome, and related multisymptom illnesses, go to http://www.publichealth.va.gov/exposures/agentorange/index.asp and http://www.publichealth.va.gov/exposures/gulfwar/index.asp. Also, consider articles on depleted uranium and the study of possible health effects addressed by McDiarmid et al. (2002).

4. EFFECTS OF COMBAT DEPLOYMENT ON SEXUAL HEALTH AND FUNCTION

1. More detailed information on the pathophysiology of sexual dysfunction can be found in Longo et al. (2011). Additionally, for a more medical context, see Kumar et al. (2014).

2. The exact number is hard to determine, but publicly available information from Brown (2011), Serkin et al. (2010), and Wood (2012) supports this estimate.

3. For more in-depth information on TBI and associated comorbidities, see Carlson et al. (2011) and Sayer (2012).

4. For a discussion of the relationship between mind and body as it relates to sexual dysfunction, see Balon (2008).

5. A great resource for understanding more about endocrinology is Silverthorn (2012): the role of hormones in the body, where they are produced, and their effects.

6. To further understand the rehabilitation process as well as outcomes from polytrauma and blast injuries, research by Sayer and her colleagues at the Veterans Administration is helpful. See Sayer et al. (2008, 2009).

7. Sayer et al. (2009) describe the impact of polytrauma and pain on injured veterans in a treatment setting. Helmer et al. (2009) describe the impact of pain on function in recent combat veterans, and Gironda et al. (2009) published some insights linking polytrauma, TBI, and pain.

8. For more information and resources regarding sexual trauma, particularly in the military, see De Silva (2001) and Street and Stafford (2014).

5. DIFFERENT IMPACT OF MILITARY SERVICE ON MEN AND WOMEN

1. More basic biological information on human sexuality, genetics, and hormones can be found in Silverthorn (2012).

2. In January 2013, Secretary of Defense Leon Panetta rescinded the policy excluding women from combat roles in the military. See Roulo (2014).

3. The U.S. Department of Veterans Affairs has created some literature providing an overview of health effects on women resulting from military service. See Batuman et al. (2011) and Murphy et al. (1997) for more insight into military women's health issues.

4. For more information on gender differences and perceptions of sex, Bem (1993) offers a thorough discussion of these subjects.

5. Stansbury et al. (2003) offer an examination of gender constructions of masculinity within the context of male veterans suffering with prostate cancer. Brown (1988) explores hypermasculinity in military culture through the experience of transgender military service members.

6. A wide array of resources and information on various aspects of military sexual trauma is available. For general information, consider Street and Stafford (2014). For female veteran–specific information on sexual harassment and domestic violence, see Murdoch et al. (1995, 1998). For information on coping strategies, see Mattocks et al. (2012). For statistics on prevalence of physical and sexual trauma, see Batuman et al. (2011), Coyle et al. (1996), Kimerling et al. (2007), and Skinner et al. (2000).

7. See Hoyt et al. (2011) for more details on the estimates of sexual trauma in male service members. Bell et al. (2014) discuss the different impact of sexual trauma on men and women.

6. THE UPS AND DOWNS
OF SEXUAL HEALTH

1. See Centers for Disease Control (2012) for more information on sexual activity among young adults in the United States.

2. More information about the demographics of the military population is available in U.S. Government Accountability Office (2005).

3. For a discussion of the normal effects of aging on sexuality, see Lichtenberg (1999). Mulligan and Moss's (1991) cross-sectional study also offers information that may be of use.

4. See Kramarow and Pastor (2012) for more details on the health of male veterans.

7. AM I NORMAL?

1. For more information about risky behaviors, including substance abuse in military personnel, consider the research of Bradley et al. (2001) and Davis and Wood (1999).

2. See Wilkinson et al. (2012) for further discussion of hormone abnormalities after TBI.

3. The bibliography contains numerous articles discussing possible medication side effects. See Baldwin (2004), Balon (2006), Fossey and Hamner (1994), Labbate et al. (1998), Lane (1997), and Montgomery et al. (2002).

4. See Smith et al. (1984).

5. To further understand trauma and its effects on sexual desire, some studies of veterans with spinal cord injuries and the effects on sexual desire and function are available; see Alexander et al. (1993). Eisenberg and Rustad (1974) provide meaningful answers to questions about sexual possibility in spinal cord injuries.

6. For more information on sex addiction, see Carnes and Adams (2013). For a discussion on motivations and desires for Internet pornography, see Paul and Shim (2008).

8. LET'S TALK ABOUT SEX

1. Linguistic anthropologist Nancy Bonvillain (2013) has a thorough book on language and communication that offers insights into how humans communicate on many levels with each other. This is of much utility within the realm of communication between intimate partners.

2. See Doss et al. (2012) and Erbes et al. (2008) for more about couples counseling for military and veteran couples.

3. For more information about AASECT and their approach to counseling and education, see http://www.aasect.org.

4. For more details on the patient–provider encounter around sexual health, see the following: Dyer and das Nair (2012), McCance et al. (1991), Moreira et al. (2005), Nusbaum and Hamilton (2002), and Rosen et al. (1993).

5. See Seal et al. (2009) and Tanielian and Jaycox (2008).

6. For more information about managing sexual side effects of medications, see Baldwin (2004), Balon (2006), Clayton and Balon (2009), and Lane (1997).

BIBLIOGRAPHY

Ahmadi, Khodabakhsh, Hossein Ranjebar-Shayan, and Fateme Raiisi. 2007. "Sexual Dysfunction and Marital Satisfaction among the Chemically Injured Veterans." *Indian Journal of Urology* 23, no. 4: 377.

Alexander, Craig J., Marca L. Sipski, and Thomas W. Findley. 1993. "Sexual Activities, Desire, and Satisfaction in Males Pre-and Post-Spinal Cord Injury." *Archives of Sexual Behavior* 22, no. 3: 217–28.

Alloggiamento, T., C. Zipp, V. K. Raxwal, E. Ashley, S. Dey, S. Levine, and V. F. Froelicher. 2001. "Sex, the Heart, and Sildenafil." *Current Problems in Cardiology* 26, no. 6: 388–415.

Anticevic, V., and D. Britvić. 2008. "Sexual Functioning in War Veterans with Posttraumatic Stress Disorder." *Croatian Medical Journal* 49, no. 4: 499–505.

Arbanas, G. 2010. "Does Post-Traumatic Stress Disorder Carry a Higher Risk of Sexual Dysfunctions?" *Journal of Sexual Medicine* 7, no. 5: 1816–21.

Baldwin, D. S. 2004. "Sexual Dysfunction Associated with Antidepressant Drugs." *Expert Opinion on Drug Safety* 3, no. 5: 457–70.

Balon, R. 2006. "SSRI-Associated Sexual Dysfunction." *American Journal of Psychiatry* 163, no. 9: 1504–0.

———, ed. 2008. *Sexual Dysfunction: The Brain-Body Connection.* Basel: Karger.

Bansal, Sudhir. 1988. "Sexual Dysfunction in Hypertensive Men: A Critical Review of the Literature." *Hypertension* 12, no. 1: 1–10.

Batuman, F., B. Bean-Mayberry, C. L. Goldzweig, C. Huang, I. M. Miake-Lye, D. L. Washington, E. M. Yano, L. C. Zephyrin, and P. G. Shekelle. 2011. *Health Effects of Military Service on Women Veterans.* VA-ESP Project 05-226. Washington, DC: Department of Veterans Affairs.

Bell, M. E., J. A. Turchik, and J. A. Karpenko. 2014. "Impact of Gender on Reactions to Military Sexual Assault and Harassment." *Health and Social Work* 39, no. 1: 25–33.

Bem, Sandra Lipsitz. 1993. *The Lenses of Gender: Transforming the Debate on Sexual Inequality.* New Haven, CT: Yale University Press.

Benedek, David M. 2010. *Clinical Manual for Management of PTSD.* Arlington, VA: American Psychiatric Publishing.

Bonvillain, Nancy. 2013. *Language, Culture, and Communication.* 7th ed. Boston: Pearson.

Bradley, K. A., K. R. Bush, T. M. Davis, D. J. Dobie, M. L. Burman, C. M. Rutter, and D. R. Kivlahan. 2001. "Binge Drinking among Female Veterans Affairs Patients: Prevalence and Associated Risks." *Psychology of Addictive Behaviors* 15, no. 4: 297–305.

Breyer, B. N., B. E. Cohen, D. Bertenthal, R. C. Rosen, T. C. Neylan, and K. H. Seal. 2014. "Sexual Dysfunction in Male Iraq and Afghanistan War Veterans: Association with Posttraumatic Stress Disorder and Other Combat-Related Mental Health Disorders: A Population-Based Cohort Study." *Journal of Sexual Medicine* 11, no. 1: 75–83.

Bronner, G., and I. Z. Ben-Zion. 2014. "Unusual Masturbatory Practice as an Etiological Factor in the Diagnosis and Treatment of Sexual Dysfunction in Young Men." *Journal of Sexual Medicine* 11, no. 7: 1798–806.

Brooks, Gary R. 2012. "Male-Sensitive Therapy for the Returning Veteran and His Partner." *Working Successfully with Men in Couples Counseling* 2012: 279.

Brown, D. 2011. "Amputations and Genital Injuries Increase Sharply among Soldiers in Afghanistan." *Washington Post.* March 4. http://www.washingtonpost.com/wp-dyn/content/article/2011/03/04/AR2011030403258.html?sid=ST2011030504659.

Brown, G. R. 1988. "Transsexuals in the Military: Flight into Hypermasculinity." *Archives of Sexual Behavior* 17, no. 6: 527–37.

Bumiller, Elisabeth. 2011. "Obama Ends 'Don't Ask, Don't Tell' Policy." *New York Times.* July 22. http://www.nytimes.com/2011/07/23/us/23military.html?_r=0.

Butterfield, M. I., and M. E. Becker. 2002. "Posttraumatic Stress Disorder in Women: Assessment and Treatment in Primary Care." *Primary Care* 29, no. 1: 151–70.

Canive, J. M., R. D. Clark, L. A. Calais, C. Qualls, and V. B. Tuason. 1998. "Bupropion Treatment in Veterans with Posttraumatic Stress Disorder: An Open Study." *Journal of Clinical Psychopharmacology* 18, no. 5: 379–83.

Carlson, K. F., S. M. Kehle, L. A. Meis, N. Greer, R. Macdonald, I. Rutks, N. A. Sayer, S. K. Dobscha, and T. J. Wilt. 2011. "Prevalence, Assessment, and Treatment of Mild Traumatic Brain Injury and Posttraumatic Stress Disorder: A Systematic Review of the Evidence." *Journal of Head Trauma Rehabilitation* 26, no. 2: 103–15.

Carnes, Patrick J., and Kenneth M. Adams. 2013. *Clinical Management of Sex Addiction.* New York: Routledge.

Centers for Disease Control. 2012. "Youth Risk Behavior Surveillance System: US, 2011." *Morbidity and Mortality Weekly Report* 61, no. 4: 1–162.

Chamie, Karim, Ralph W. deVere White, Dennis Lee, Joonha Ok, and Lars M. Ellison. 2008. "Agent Orange Exposure, Vietnam War Veterans, and the Risk of Prostate Cancer." *Cancer* 113, no. 9: 2464–70.

Chu, David S. C. 2011. "Qualification Standards for Enlistment, Appointment, and Induction." September 20, 2005, Change 2.—9/20/2011. U.S. Department of Defense Memorandum. September 20.

Chung, Moon Yong, Kyung Ho Min, Yong Ju Jun, Sung Soo Kim, Wan Chul Kim, and Eun Mi Jun. 2004. "Efficacy and Tolerability of Mirtazapine and Sertraline in Korean Veterans with Posttraumatic Stress Disorder: A Randomized Open Label Trial." *Human Psychopharmacology: Clinical and Experimental* 19, no. 7: 489–94.

Cifu, D. X., B. C. Taylor, W. F. Carne, D. Bidelspach, N. A. Sayer, J. Scholten, and E. H. Campbell. 2013. "Traumatic Brain Injury, Posttraumatic Stress Disorder, and Pain Diagnoses in OIF/OEF/OND Veterans." *Journal of Rehabilitation Research and Development* 50, no. 9: 1169–76.

Clayton, A. H., and R. Balon. 2009. "The Impact of Mental Illness and Psychotropic Medications on Sexual Functioning: The Evidence and Management." *Journal of Sexual Medicine* 6: 1200–1211.

Cohen, B. E., S. Maguen, D. Bertenthal, Y. Shi, V. Jacoby, and K. H. Seal. 2012. "Reproductive and Other Health Outcomes in Iraq and Afghanistan Women Veterans Using VA Health Care: Association with Mental Health Diagnoses." *Women's Health Issues* 22, no. 5: e461–71.

Coyle, B. S., D. L. Wolan, and A. S. Van Horn. 1996. "The Prevalence of Physical and Sexual Abuse in Women Veterans Seeking Care at a Veterans Affairs Medical Center." *Military Medicine* 161, no. 10: 588–93.

Davis, T. M., and P. S. Wood. 1999. "Substance Abuse and Sexual Trauma in a Female Veteran Population." *Journal of Substance Abuse Treatment* 16, no. 2: 123–27.

De Silva, Padmal. 2001. "Impact of Trauma on Sexual Functioning and Sexual Relationships." *Sexual and Relationship Therapy* 16, no. 3: 269–78.

Dobkin, Bruce H. 2003. *The Clinical Science of Neurologic Rehabilitation*. Oxford: Oxford University Press.

Doss, Brian D., Lorelei Simpson Rowe, Kristen R. Morrison, Julian Libet, Gary R. Birchler, Joshua W. Madsen, and John R. McQuaid. 2012. "Couple Therapy for Military Veterans: Overall Effectiveness and Predictors of Response." *Behavior Therapy* 43, no. 1: 216–27.

Düsing, Rainer. 2005. "Sexual Dysfunction in Male Patients with Hypertension." *Drugs* 65, no. 6: 773–86.

Dyer, K., and R. das Nair. (2012). "Why Don't Healthcare Professionals Talk about Sex? A Systematic Review of Recent Qualitative Studies Conducted in the United Kingdom." *Journal of Sexual Medicine* 10, no. 11: 2658–70.

Eisenberg, Myron G., and L. C. Rustad. 1974. *Sex and the Spinal Cord Injured: Some Questions and Answers*. Cleveland, OH: Veterans Administration Hospital.

Elhai, J. D., B. C. Frueh, P. B. Gold, S. N. Gold, and M. B. Hamner. 2000. "Clinical Presentations of Posttraumatic Stress Disorder across Trauma Populations: A Comparison of MMPI-2 Profiles of Combat Veterans and Adult Survivors of Child Sexual Abuse." *Journal of Nervous and Mental Disease* 188, no. 10: 708–13.

Erbes, Christopher R., Melissa A. Polusny, Shelley MacDermid, and Jill S. Compton. 2008. "Couple Therapy with Combat Veterans and Their Partners." *Journal of Clinical Psychology* 64, no. 8: 972–83.

Finger, William W., Margaret Lund, and Mark A. Slagle. 1997. "Medications That May Contribute to Sexual Disorders. A Guide to Assessment and Treatment in Family Practice." *Journal of Family Practice* 44, no. 1: 33–43.

Fischer, Hannah. 2004. *A Guide to U.S. Military Casualty Statistics: Operation New Dawn, Operation Iraqi Freedom, and Operation Enduring Freedom*. Washington, DC: Congressional Research Service.

Fontana, A., L. S. Schwartz, and R. Rosenheck. 1997. "Posttraumatic Stress Disorder among Female Vietnam Veterans: A Causal Model of Etiology." *American Journal of Public Health* 87, no. 2: 169–75.

Fossey, M. D., and M. B. Hamner. 1994. "Clonazepam-Related Sexual Dysfunction in Male Veterans with PTSD." *Anxiety* 1, no. 5: 233–36.

Frank, Ellen, Carol Anderson, and Debra Rubinstein. 1978. "Frequency of Sexual Dysfunction in Normal Couples." *New England Journal of Medicine* 299, no. 3: 111–15.

Frayne, S. M., K. M. Skinner, L. M. Sullivan, T. J. Tripp, C. S. Hankin, N. R. Kressin, and D. R. Miller. 1999. "Medical Profile of Women Veterans Administration Outpatients Who Report a History of Sexual Assault Occurring while in the Military." *Journal of Women's Health and Gender-Based Medicine* 8, no. 6: 835–45.

Friedemann-Sanchez, Greta, Nina A. Sayer, and Treven Pickett. 2008. "Provider Perspectives on Rehabilitation of Patients with Polytrauma." *Archives of Physical Medicine and Rehabilitation* 89, no. 1: 171–78.

Friedman, M. J., P. P. Schnurr, and A. McDonagh-Coyle. 1994. "Post-Traumatic Stress Disorder in the Military Veteran." *Psychiatric Clinics of North America* 17, no. 2: 265–77.

Frueh, B. Christopher, Samuel M. Turner, Deborah C. Beidel, and Shawn P. Cahill. 2001. "Assessment of Social Functioning in Combat Veterans with PTSD." *Aggression and Violent Behavior* 6, no. 1: 79–90.

Fugl-Meyer, A. R., G. Lodnert, I. B. Branholm, and K. S. Fugl-Meyer. 1997. "On Life Satisfaction in Male Erectile Dysfunction." *International Journal of Impotence Research* 9: 141–48.

Gades, Naomi M., Ajay Nehra, Debra J. Jacobson, Michaela E. McGree, Cynthia J. Girman, Thomas Rhodes, Rosebud O. Roberts, Michael M. Lieber, and Steven J. Jacobsen. 2005. "Association between Smoking and Erectile Dysfunction: A Population-Based Study." *American Journal of Epidemiology* 161, no. 4: 346–51.

Gallagher, J. G., D. S. Riggs, C. A. Byrne, and F. W. Weathers. 1998. "Female Partners' Estimations of Male Veterans' Combat-Related PTSD Severity." *Journal of Traumatic Stress* 11, no. 2: 367–74.

Gilhooly, Patricia E., John E. Ottenweller, Gudrun Lange, Lana Tiersky, and Benjamin H. Natelson. 2001. "Chronic Fatigue and Sexual Dysfunction in Female Gulf War Veterans." *Journal of Sex and Marital Therapy* 27, no. 5: 483–87.

Gironda, R. J., M. E. Clark, R. L. Ruff, S. Chait, M. Craine, R. Walker, and J. Scholten. 2009. "Traumatic Brain Injury, Polytrauma, and Pain: Challenges and Treatment Strategies for the Polytrauma Rehabilitation." *Rehabilitation Psychology* 54, no. 3: 247–58.

Goyal, V., K. Mattocks, E. B. Schwarz, S. Borrero, M. Skanderson, L. Zephyrin, C. Brandt, and S. Haskell. 2014. "Contraceptive Provision in the VA Healthcare System to Women Who Report Military Sexual Trauma." *Journal of Women's Health.* May, Epub ahead of print. http://www.ncbi.nlm.nih.gov/pubmed/24787680.

Gronseth, Gary S. 2005. "Gulf War Syndrome: A Toxic Exposure? A Systematic Review." *Neurologic Clinics* 23, no. 2: 523–40.

Helmer, Drew A., Greg Beaulieu, Cheryl Houlette, David M. Latini, Heather H. Goltz, Samuel Etienne, and Michael Kauth. 2013. "Assessment and Documentation of Sexual Health Issues of Recent Combat Veterans Seeking VHA Care." *Journal of Sexual Medicine* 10, no. 4: 1065–73.

Helmer, Drew A., H. K. Chandler, K. S. Quigley, M. Blatt, R. Teichman, and G. Lange. 2009. "Chronic Widespread Pain, Mental Health, and Physical Role Function in OEF/OIF Veterans." *Pain Medicine* 10, no. 7: 1174–82.

Hirsch, Kenneth A. 2009. "Sexual Dysfunction in Male Operation Enduring Freedom/Operation Iraqi Freedom Patients with Severe Post-Traumatic Stress Disorder." *Military Medicine* 174, no. 5: 520–22.

Hirshkowitz, Max, Murat O. Arcasoy, Ismet Karacan, Robert L. Williams, and James W. Howell. 1992. "Nocturnal Penile Tumescence in Cigarette Smokers with Erectile Dysfunction." *Urology* 39, no. 2: 101–7.

Holmes-Eber, Paula. 2014. *Culture in Conflict: Irregular Warfare, Culture Policy, and the Marine Corps.* Stanford, CA: Stanford University Press.

Hosain, G. Manawar, David M. Latini, Michael Kauth, Heather H. Goltz, and Drew A. Helmer. 2013. "Racial Differences in Sexual Dysfunction among Postdeployed Iraq and Afghanistan Veterans." *American Journal of Men's Health* 7, no. 5: 374–81.

———. 2013. "Sexual Dysfunction among Male Veterans Returning from Iraq and Afghanistan: Prevalence and Correlates." *Journal of Sexual Medicine* 10, no. 2: 516–23.

Hoyt, T., J. Klosterman Rielage, and L. F. Williams. 2011. "Military Sexual Trauma in Men: A Review of Reported Rates." *Journal of Trauma and Dissociation* 12, no. 3: 244–60.

Iowa Persian Gulf Study Group. 1997. "Self-Reported Illness and Health Status among Gulf War Veterans. A Population-Based Study.." *Journal of the American Medical Association* 277, no. 3: 238–45.

Ishøy, T., Anna-Maria Andersson, Poul Suadicani, Bernadette Guldager, Merete Appleyard, Finn Gyntelberg, and Niels Erik Skakkebæk. 2001. "Major Reproductive Health Characteristics in Male Gulf War Veterans: The Danish Gulf War Study." *Danish Medical Bulletin* 48, no. 1: 29–32.

Ismail, Khalida, and Glyn Lewis. 2006. "Multi-Symptom Illnesses, Unexplained Illness and Gulf War Syndrome." *Philosophical Transactions of the Royal Society B: Biological Sciences* 361, no. 1468: 543–51.

Jaffe, Greg. 2014. "Cold Calculations: How a Backlogged VA Determines the True Cost of War." *After the Wars.* http://www.washingtonpost.com/sf/national/2014/05/20/after-the-wars-cold-calculations/?hpid=z2.

Jamshid, A., and M. D. Marvasti. 2004. *Psychiatric Treatment of Victims and Survivors of Sexual Trauma: A Neuro-Bio-Psychological Approach.* Springfield, IL: Charles C Thomas.

Kaplan, Peter M. 1989. "Post-Traumatic Stress Syndrome and Sexual Dysfunction." *Journal of Sex and Marital Therapy* 15, no. 1: 74–77.

Katz, Lori S., G. Cojucar, S. Beheshti, E. Nakamura, and M. Murray. 2012. "Military Sexual Trauma during Deployment to Iraq and Afghanistan: Prevalence, Readjustment, and Gender Differences." *Violence and Victims* 27, no. 4: 487–99.

Kauth, M. R., C. Meier, and D. M. Latini. 2014. "A Review of Sexual Health among Lesbian, Gay, and Bisexual Veterans." *Current Sexual Health Reports* 6, no. 2: 106–13.

Kessler, R. C., S. G. Heeringa, M. B. Stein, L. J. Colpe, C. S. Fullerton, I. Hwang, J. A. Naifeh, M. K. Nock, M. Petukhova, N. A. Sampson, M. Schoenbaum, A. M. Zaslavsky, and R. J. Ursano. 2014. "Thirty-Day Prevalence of DSM-IV Mental Disorders among Nondeployed Soldiers in the US Army: Results from the Army Study to Assess Risk and Resilience in Servicemembers (Army STARRS)." *JAMA Psychiatry* 71, no. 5: 504–13.

Kim, Hyoung-Ah, Eun-Mi Kim, Yeong-Chul Park, Ji-Yeon Yu, Seung-Kwon Hong, Seong-Hoon Jeon, Kui-Lea Park, Sook-Jin Hur, and Yong Heo. 2003. "Immunotoxicological Effects of Agent Orange Exposure to the Vietnam War Korean Veterans." *Industrial Health* 41, no. 3. 158–66.

Kimerling, Rachel, Kristian Gima, Mark W. Smith, Amy Street, and Susan Frayne. 2007. "The Veterans Health Administration and Military Sexual Trauma." *American Journal of Public Health* 97, no. 12: 2160–66.

Kostanjsek, N. 2011. "Use of the International Classification of Functioning, Disability and Health (ICF) as a Conceptual Framework and Common Language for Disability Statistics and Health Information Systems." *BMC Public Health* 11, suppl. 4: S3.

Kotler, M., H. Cohen, D. Aizenberg, M. Matar, U. Loewenthal, Z. Kaplan, H. Miodownik, and Z. Zemishlany. 2000. "Sexual Dysfunction in Male Posttraumatic Stress Disorder Patients." *Psychotherapy and Psychosomatics* 69: 309–15.

Kramarow, E. A., and P. N. Pastor. 2012. "The Health of Male Veterans and Nonveterans Aged 25–64: United States, 2007–2010." NCHS Data Brief no. 101. Hyattsville, MD: National Center for Health Statistics.

Kumar, Vinay, Abul Abbas, and John Aster. 2014. *Robbins and Cotran Pathologic Basis of Disease.* 9th ed. Philadelphia: Saunders/Elsevier.

Labbate, Lawrence A., Jamie Grimes, Alan Hiaes, Marvin A. Oleshansky, and George W. Arana. 1998. "Sexual Dysfunction Induced by Serotonin Reuptake Antidepressants." *Journal of Sex and Marital Therapy* 24, no. 1: 3–12.

Lange, Gudrun. 2011. "Gulf War Syndrome." In *Encyclopedia of Clinical Neuropsychology.* New York: Springer.

Lane, R. M. 1997. "A Critical Review of Selective Serotonin Reuptake Inhibitor-Related Sexual Dysfunction: Incidence, Possible Aetiology and Implications for Management." *Journal of Psychopharmacology* 11, no. 1: 72–82.

Latini, David M., David F. Penson, Katrine L. Wallace, Deborah P. Lubeck, and Tom F. Lue. 2006. "Original Research—Erectile Dysfunction: Clinical and Psychosocial Characteristics of Men with Erectile Dysfunction: Baseline Data from Exceed™." *Journal of Sexual Medicine* 3, no. 6: 1059–67.

Laumann, E. O., A. Paik, and R. C. Rosen. 1999. "Sexual Dysfunction in the United States: Prevalence and Predictors." *Journal of the American Medical Association* 281: 537–44.

Laurent, Sean M., and Anne D. Simons. 2009. "Sexual Dysfunction in Depression and Anxiety: Conceptualizing Sexual Dysfunction as Part of an Internalizing Dimension." *Clinical Psychology Review* 29, no. 7: 573–85.

Lehavot, K., J. G. Katon, E. C. Williams, K. M. Nelson, C. M. Gardella, G. E. Reiber, and T. L. Simpson. 2014. "Sexual Behaviors and Sexually Transmitted Infections in a Nationally Representative Sample of Women Veterans and Nonveterans." *Journal of Women's Health* 23, no. 3: 246–52.

Letourneau, E. J., P. A. Schewe, and B. C. Frueh. 1997. "Preliminary Evaluation of Sexual Problems in Combat Veterans with PTSD." *Journal of Traumatic Stress* 10, no. 1: 125–32.

Lichtenberg, Peter A. 1999. *Handbook of Assessment in Clinical Gerontology.* New York: Wiley, 1999.

Litwin, Mark S., Robert J. Nied, and Nasreen Dhanani. 1998. "Health-Related Quality of Life in Men with Erectile Dysfunction." *Journal of General Internal Medicine* 13, no. 3: 159–66.

Longo, Dan, Anthony Fauci, Dennis Kasper, Stephen Hauser, J. Jameson, and Joseph Loscalzo. 2011. *Harrison's Principles of Internal Medicine: Volumes 1 and 2.* 18th ed. New York: McGraw-Hill.

Mannino, David M., R. Monina Klevens, and W. Dana Flanders. 1994. "Cigarette Smoking: An Independent Risk Factor for Impotence?" *American Journal of Epidemiology* 140, no. 11: 1003–8.

Markle, W., T. Conti, and M. Kad. 2013. "Sexually Transmitted Diseases." *Primary Care* 40, no. 3: 557–87.

Martin, B. R. 2002. "Counseling Patients about Sexual Dysfunction." *Journal of the American Pharmaceutical Association* 42, no. 2: 352, 354.

Masters, W. H., and Virginia E. Johnson. 1966. *Human Sexual Response.* New York: Bantam.

Mattocks, Kristin M., Sally G. Haskell, Erin E. Krebs, Amy C. Justice, Elizabeth M. Yano, and Cynthia Brandt. 2012. "Women at War: Understanding How Women Veterans Cope with Combat and Military Sexual Trauma." *Social Science and Medicine* 74, no. 4: 537–45.

McCance, K. L., R. Moser, and K. R. Smith. 1991. "A Survey of Physicians' Knowledge and Application of AIDS Prevention Capabilities." *American Journal of Preventive Medicine* 7, no. 3: 141–45.

McDiarmid, M. A., F. J. Hooper, K. Squibb, K. McPhaul, S. M. Engelhardt, R. Kane, R. DiPino, and M. Kabat. 2002. "Health Effects and Biological Monitoring Results of Gulf War Veterans Exposed to Depleted Uranium." *Military Medicine* 167, no. 2 (suppl.): 123–24.

McIntyre, L. M., M. I. Butterfield, K. Nanda, K. Parsey, K. M. Stechuchak, A. W. McChesney, C. Koons, and L. A. Bastian. 1999. "Validation of a Trauma Questionnaire in Veteran Women." *Journal of General Internal Medicine* 14, no. 3: 186–89.

McVary, Kevin T., Serge Carrier, and Hunter Wessells. 2001. "Smoking and Erectile Dysfunction: Evidence Based Analysis." *Journal of Urology* 166, no. 5: 1624–32.

Meston, C. M., and P. F. Frohlich. 2000. "The Neurobiology of Sexual Function." *Archives of General Psychiatry* 57: 1012–30.

Miller, Bruce L., Jeffrey L. Cummings, Hugh McIntyre, George Ebers, and M. Grode. 1986. "Hypersexuality or Altered Sexual Preference Following Brain Injury." *Journal of Neurology, Neurosurgery, and Psychiatry* 49, no. 8: 867–73.

Miller, J. L. 2000. "Post-Traumatic Stress Disorder in Primary Care Practice." *Journal of the American Academy of Nurse Practitioners* 12, no. 11: 475–82.

Modelska, Katharina, and Steven Cummings. 2003. "Female Sexual Dysfunction in Postmenopausal Women: Systematic Review of Placebo-Controlled Trials." *American Journal of Obstetrics and Gynecology* 188, no. 1: 286–93.

Monson, Candice M., Steffany J. Fredman, and Kathryn C. Adair. 2008. "Cognitive–Behavioral Conjoint Therapy for Posttraumatic Stress Disorder: Application to Operation Enduring and Iraqi Freedom Veterans." *Journal of Clinical Psychology* 64, no. 8: 958–71.

Montgomery, S. A., D. S. Baldwin, and A. Riley. 2002. "Antidepressant Medications: A Review of the Evidence for Drug-Induced Sexual Dysfunction." *Journal of Affective Disorders* 69: 119–40.

Moore, Keith, T. V. N. Persaud, and Mark Torchia. 2011. *The Developing Human: Clinically Oriented Embryology.* 9th ed. Philadelphia: Saunders/Elsevier.

Moreira, E. D., G. Brock, D. B. Glasser, A. Nicolosi, E. O. Laumann, A. Paik, and C. Gingell. 2005. "Help-Seeking Behaviour for Sexual Problems: The Global Study of Sexual Attitudes and Behaviors." *International Journal of Clinical Practice* 59, no. 1: 6–16.

Morley, John E. 1986. "Impotence." *American Journal of Medicine* 80, no. 5: 897–905.

Mulligan, Thomas, and C. Renee Moss. 1991. "Sexuality and Aging in Male Veterans: A Cross-Sectional Study of Interest, Ability, and Activity." *Archives of Sexual Behavior* 20, no. 1: 17–25.

Murdoch, M., and P. G. McGovern. 1998. "Measuring Sexual Harassment: Development and Validation of the Sexual Harassment Inventory." *Violence and Victims* 13, no. 3: 203–16.

Murdoch, M., and K. L. Nichol. 1995. "Women Veterans' Experiences with Domestic Violence and with Sexual Harassment while in the Military." *Archives of Family Medicine* 4, no. 5: 411–18.

Murphy, F., D. Browne, S. Mather, H. Scheele, and K. C. Hyams. 1997. "Women in the Persian Gulf War: Health Care Implications for Active Duty Troops and Veterans." *Military Medicine* 162, no. 10: 656–60.

Mustafa, Masroor, Nkolika Erokwu, Idowa Ebose, and Kingman Strohl. 2005. "Sleep Problems and the Risk for Sleep Disorders in an Outpatient Veteran Population." *Sleep and Breathing* 9, no. 2: 57–63.

Netter, Frank. 2014. *Atlas of Human Anatomy*. 6th ed. Philadelphia: Saunders/Elsevier.

Nock, M. K., M. B. Stein, S. G. Heeringa, R. J. Ursano, L. J. Colpe, C. S. Fullerton, I. Hwang, J. A. Naifeh, N. A. Sampson, M. Schoenbaum, A. M. Zaslavsky, and R. C. Kessler. 2014. "Prevalence and Correlates of Suicidal Behavior among Soldiers: Results from the Army Study to Assess Risk and Resilience in Servicemembers (Army STARRS)." *JAMA Psychiatry* 71, no. 5: 514–22.

Nolan, Bruce. 1995. "Sleep Events among Veterans with Combat-Related Posttraumatic Stress Disorder." *American Journal of Psychiatry* 1: 52.

Nusbaum, Margaret R. H., and Carol D. Hamilton. 2002. "The Proactive Sexual Health History." *American Family Physician* 66: 1705–12.

Nussbaum, Robert, Roderick McInnes, and Huntington Willard. 2007. *Thompson and Thompson Genetics in Medicine*. 7th ed. Philadelphia: Saunders/Elsevier.

Orr, Guy, Mark Weiser, Michael Polliack, Gil Raviv, Daphne Tadmor, and Leon Grunhaus. 2006. "Effectiveness of Sildenafil in Treating Erectile Dysfunction in PTSD Patients: A Double-Blind, Placebo-Controlled Crossover Study." *Journal of Clinical Psychopharmacology* 26, no. 4: 426–30.

Paul, Bryant, and Jae Woong Shim. 2008. "Gender, Sexual Affect, and Motivations for Internet Pornography Use." *International Journal of Sexual Health* 20, no. 3: 187–99.

Pierce, P. F. 1997. "Physical and Emotional Health of Gulf War Veteran Women." *Aviation. Space, and Environmental Medicine* 68, no. 4: 317–21.

Prisant, L. Michael, Albert A. Carr, Peter B. Bottini, Diane S. Solursh, and Lionel P. Solursh. 1994. "Sexual Dysfunction with Antihypertensive Drugs." *Archives of Internal Medicine* 154, no. 7: 730–36.

Pugh, M. J., E. P. Finley, L. A. Copeland, C. P. Wang, P. H. Noel, M. E. Amuan, H. M. Parsons, M. Wells, B. Elizondo, and J. A. Pugh. 2014 "Complex Comorbidity Clusters in OEF/OIF Veterans: The Polytrauma Clinical Triad and Beyond." *Medical Care* 52, no. 2: 172–81.

Ramchand, R., T. L. Schell, B. R. Karney, K. C. Osilla, R. M. Burns, and L. B. Caldarone. 2010. "Disparate Prevalence Estimates of PTSD among Service Members Who Served in Iraq and Afghanistan: Possible Explanations." *Journal of Traumatic Stress* 23: 59–68.

Recognize the Sacrifice. 2014. "Purple Heart Criteria." http://www.recognizethesacrifice.org/purple-heart-criteria.html.

Resnick, E. M., M. Mallampalli, and C. L. Carter. 2012. "Current Challenges in Female Veterans' Health." *Journal of Women's Health* 21, no. 9: 895–900.

Rosen, R. C., J. F. Taylor, S. R. Leiblum, and G. A. Bachmann. 1993. "Prevalence of Sexual Dysfunction in Women: Results of a Survey Study of 329 Women in an Outpatient Gynecological Clinic." *Journal of Sex and Marital Therapy* 19: 171–88.

Ross, Richard J., William A. Ball, David F. Dinges, Nancy B. Kribbs, Adrian R. Morrison, Steven M. Silver, and Francis D. Mulvaney. 1994. "Rapid Eye Movement Sleep Disturbance in Posttraumatic Stress Disorder." *Biological Psychiatry* 35, no. 3: 195–202.

Roulo, Claudette. 2014. "Defense Department Expands Women's Combat Role." http://www.defense.gov/news/newsarticle.aspx?id=119098.

Sanchez-Cruz, J. J., A. Cabrera-Leon, A. Martin-Morales, A. Fernandez, R. Burgos, and J. Rejas. 2003. "Male Erectile Dysfunction and Health-Related Quality of Life." *European Urology* 44, no. 2: 245–53.

Sayer, Nina A. 2012. "Traumatic Brain Injury and Its Neuropsychiatric Sequelae in War Veterans." *Annual Review of Medicine* 63: 405–19.

Sayer, Nina A., Christine E. Chiros, Barbara Sigford, Steven Scott, Barbara Clothier, Treven Pickett, and Henry L. Lew. 2008. "Characteristics and Rehabilitation Outcomes among

Patients with Blast and Other Injuries Sustained during the Global War on Terror." *Archives of Physical Medicine and Rehabilitation* 89, no. 1: 163–70.

Sayer, Nina A., David X. Cifu, Shane McNamee, Christine E. Chiros, Barbara J. Sigford, Steve Scott, and Henry L. Lew. 2009. "Rehabilitation Needs of Combat-Injured Service Members Admitted to the VA Polytrauma Rehabilitation Centers: The Role of PM&R in the Care of Wounded Warriors." *PM&R* 1, no. 1: 23–28.

Sayer, Nina A., S. Noorbaloochi, P. Frazier, K. Carlson, A. Gravely, and M. Murdoch. 2010. "Reintegration Problems and Treatment Interests among Iraq and Afghanistan Combat Veterans Receiving VA Medical Care." *Psychiatric Services* 61, no. 6: 589–97.

Schecter, Arnold, Harry McGee, John S. Stanley, Kathy Boggess, and Paul Brandt-Rauf. 1996. "Dioxins and Dioxin-Like Chemicals in Blood and Semen of American Vietnam Veterans from the State of Michigan." *American Journal of Industrial Medicine* 30, no. 6: 647–54.

Schmidt, H. M., T. Munder, H. Gerger, S. Fruhauf, and J. Barth. 2014. "Combination of Psychological Intervention and Phosphodiesterase-5 Inhibitors for Erectile Dysfunction: A Narrative Review and Meta-Analysis." *Journal of Sexual Medicine* 11, no. 6: 1376–91.

Schnurr, P. P., D. Kaloupek, N. Sayer, D. S. Weiss, J. Cohen, S. Galea, et al. 2010. "Understanding the Impact of the Wars in Iraq and Afghanistan." *Journal of Traumatic Stress* 23: 3–4.

Schoenbaum, M., R. C. Kessler, S. E. Gilman, L. J. Colpe, S. G. Heeringa, M. B. Stein, R. J. Ursano, and K. L. Cox. 2014. "Predictors of Suicide and Accident Death in the Army Study to Assess Risk and Resilience in Servicemembers (Army STARRS): Results from the Army Study to Assess Risk and Resilience in Servicemembers (Army STARRS)." *JAMA Psychiatry* 71, no. 5: 493–503.

Seal, K. H., T. J. Metzler, K. S. Gima, D. Bertenthal, S. Maguen, and C. S. Marmar. 2009. "Trends and Risk Factors for Mental Health Diagnoses among Iraq and Afghanistan Veterans Using Department of Veterans Affairs Health Care, 2002–2008." *American Journal of Public Health* 99, no. 9: 1651–58.

Secretary of the Army to Principal Officials of Headquarters, Department of the Army. 2012. "Army Directive 2012–16 (Changes to Army Policy for the Assignment of Female Soldiers)." Memorandum. June 27.

Serkin, F. B., D. W. Soderdahl, J. Hernandez, M. Patterson, L. Blackbourne, and C. E. Wade. 2010. "Combat Urologic Trauma in US Military Overseas Contingency Operations." *Journal of Trauma* 69, suppl. 1: S175–78.

Servicemembers Legal Defense Network. 2011. *Freedom to Serve: The Definitive Guide to LGBT Service*. Washington, DC: Servicemembers Legal Defense Network.

Silverthorn, Dee Unglaub. 2012. *Human Physiology: An Integrated Approach Plus Mastering A&P with eText—Access Card Package*. 6th ed. Boston: Pearson.

Skinner, Katherine M., Nancy Kressin, Susan Frayne, Tara J. Tripp, Cheryl S. Hankin, Donald R. Miller, and Lisa M. Sullivan. 2000. "The Prevalence of Military Sexual Assault among Female Veterans' Administration Outpatients." *Journal of Interpersonal Violence* 15, no. 3: 291–310.

Smith, David E., Donald R. Wesson, and Mickey Apter-Marsh. 1984. "Cocaine- and Alcohol-Induced Sexual Dysfunction in Patients with Addictive Disease." *Journal of Psychoactive Drugs* 16, no. 4: 359–61.

Solomon, Zahava, Shimrit Debby-Aharon, Gadi Zerach, and Danny Horesh. 2011. "Marital Adjustment, Parental Functioning, and Emotional Sharing in War Veterans." *Journal of Family Issues* 32, no. 1: 127–47.

Solursh, Lionel P., and Diane S. Solursh. 1994. "Male Erectile Disorders in Vietnam Combat Veterans with Chronic Post-Traumatic Stress Disorder." *International Journal of Adolescent Medicine and Health* 7, no. 2: 119–24.

Stahlman, S., M. Javanbakht, S. Cochran, A. B. Hamilton, S. Shoptaw, and P. M. Gorbach. 2014. "Self-Reported Sexually Transmitted Infections and Sexual Risk Behaviors in the US Military: How Sex Influences Risk." *Sexually Transmitted Diseases* 41, no. 6: 359–64.

Stansbury, James P., Marianne Mathewson-Chapman, and Kathryn E. Grant. 2003. "Gender Schema and Prostate Cancer: Veterans' Cultural Model of Masculinity." *Medical Anthropology* 22, no. 2: 175–204.

Street, Amy, and Jane Stafford. 2014. "Military Sexual Trauma: Issues in Caring for Veterans." http://www.ncptsd.org//war/military_sexual_trauma.html.

Tampi, Rajesh R., Sunanda Muralee, and Natalie D. Weder. 2008. *Comprehensive Review of Psychiatry*. Philadelphia: Lippincott Williams & Wilkins.

Tanielian, T., and L. H. Jaycox. 2008. *Invisible Wounds of War: Psychological and Cognitive Injuries, Their Consequences, and Services to Assist Recovery*. Santa Monica, CA: RAND Corporation.

Taylor, M. J. 2006. "Strategies for Managing Antidepressant-Induced Sexual Dysfunction: A Review." *Current Psychiatry Reports* 8, no. 6: 431–36.

U.S. Congress. 2013. "10 U.S. Code Chapter 47—Uniform Code of Military Justice." http://www.law.cornell.edu/uscode/text/10/subtitle-A/part-II/chapter-47.

U.S. Department of Defense. 2012. *Manual for Courts-Martial (MCM), United States*. Washington, DC: Government Printing Office.

U.S. Department of Veterans Affairs, Office of Public Affairs. 2014. *America's Wars*. http://www.va.gov/opa/publications/factsheets/fs_americas_wars.pdf.

U.S. Department of Veterans Affairs, Veterans Health Administration. 2014. *Health Care Benefits Overview 2012*. http://www.va.gov/healthbenefits/resources/publications/IB10-185-health_care_benefits_overview_2012_eng.pdf.

U.S. Department of Veterans Affairs, Veterans Health Administration, Office of Public Health. 2014. "Agent Orange." http://www.publichealth.va.gov/exposures/agentorange/index.asp.

———. 2014. "Gulf War Veterans' Illnesses." http://www.publichealth.va.gov/exposures/gulfwar/index.asp.

U.S. Department of Veterans Affairs, Veterans Health Administration, Office of Public Health, Post-Deployment Health Group, Epidemiology Division. 2014. "VA Health Care Utilization among OEF/OIF/OND Veterans Cumulative from 1st Qtr FY 2002–1st Qtr FY 2014." March.

U.S. Government Accountability Office. 2005. "Military Personnel: Reporting Additional Servicemember Demographics Could Enhance Congressional Oversight (GAO-05-952)." http://www.gao.gov/products/GAO-05-952. September.

Vermeulen, Ruud C. W., and Hans R. Scholte. 2004. "Chronic Fatigue Syndrome and Sexual Dysfunction." *Journal of Psychosomatic Research* 56, no. 2: 199–201.

Waite, L. J., E. O. Laumann, A. Das, and L. P. Schumm. 2009. "Sexuality: Measures of Partnerships, Practices, Attitudes, and Problems in the National Social Life, Health, and Aging Study." *Journal of Gerontology Series B: Psychological Sciences and Social Sciences* 64, suppl. 1: i56–66.

Westerink, Jan, and Leah Giarratano. 1999. "The Impact of Posttraumatic Stress Disorder on Partners and Children of Australian Vietnam Veterans." *Australian and New Zealand Journal of Psychiatry* 33, no. 6: 841–47.

Wilkeson, A., M. T. Lambert, and F. Petty. 2000. "Posttraumatic Stress Disorder, Dissociation, and Trauma Exposure in Depressed and Nondepressed Veterans." *Journal of Nervous and Mental Disease* 188, no. 8: 505–9.

Wilkinson, C. W., K. F. Pagulayan, E. C. Petrie, C. L. Mayer, E. A. Colasurdo, J. B. Shofer, K. L. Hart, D. Hoff, M. A. Tarabochia, and E. R. Peskind. 2012. "High Prevalence of Chronic Pituitary and Target-Organ Hormone Abnormalities after Blast-Related Mild Traumatic Brain Injury." *Frontiers in Neurology* 3: 11.

Wolfe, J. 1996. "Posttraumatic Stress Disorder in Women Veterans." *Women's Health Issues* 6, no. 6: 349–52.

Wood, David. 2012. "Afghanistan Veterans with Genital Wounds Receive Little Help from Pentagon." *Huffington Post*. July 30. http://www.huffingtonpost.com/2012/07/30/afghanistan-veterans-genital-wounds_n_1719896.html.

World Health Organization. 2014. "WHO Definition of Health." Preamble to the Constitution of the World Health Organization as Adopted by the International Health Confer-

ence, New York, June 19–22, 1946; signed on July 22, 1946, by the representatives of 61
    States (Official Records of the World Health Organization, no. 2, p. 100) and Entered into
    Force on April 7, 1948. http://www.who.int/about/definition/en/print.html.
Zemishlany, Zvi, and Abraham Weizman. 2008. "The Impact of Mental Illness on Sexual
    Dysfunction." *Advances in Psychosomatic Medicine* 29: 89–106.
Zohar, J., and H. G. M. Westenberg. 2000. "Anxiety Disorders: A Review of Tricyclic Antide-
    pressants and Selective Serotonin Reuptake Inhibitors." *Acta Psychiatrica Scandinavica*
    101, no. S403: 39–49.

INDEX

AASECT. *See* American Association of Sexuality Educators, Counselors, and Therapists

abuse. *See* sexual abuse

Agent Orange, 41–42; combat deployment effects of, 59–60; Steve and, 42

alcohol, 37, 56; Clarissa and, 57; inhibition loss when using, 57; Julio and, 57

American Association of Sexuality Educators, Counselors, and Therapists (AASECT), 120

anal sex, 5

anxiety, 13

arousal: hyperarousal, 33; Jack and, 101; Juan and, 101; normal and, 100–101; sexual response cycle and, 10, 100–101; women and, 101

balance, 93–94

baseline desire: cognitive component of, 8–9; depression and, 54; Edward and, 47; hormones and, 8; Joe and, 49; Jonah and, 96; normal, 96–98; sexual health and, 8–9; sleep disruption and, 58

beta-blockers, 56

binge drinking, 21

biopsychosocial approach, 3

boredom, 100

brain: climax and, 11; desire and, 10; mild TBI and, 47–48; PTSD and, 32–35. *See also* traumatic brain injury (TBI)

cardiovascular disease, 60

celibacy, 7

chromosomes, 63

chronic multisymptom illness, 40; combat deployment effects, 59

Clarissa, xii; alcohol and, 57; back injury of, 28, 50–51; physiatrist and, 134; polytrauma and, 50–51; risky behavior of, 97; structural challenges of, 105

clergy and chaplains, 122–123

climax: brain and, 11; Joe and Megan and, 102; normal and, 101–103; sexual response cycle and, 11, 101–103; SSRIs and, 102–103; Tom and Lisa and, 102–103

combat deployment effects: of Agent Orange, 59–60; chronic multisymptom illness, 59; depression, 36, 54–55; genital injuries, 46; Gulf War illness, 39–40, 59; invisible war wounds, 28–39; medication adverse effects, 55–56; occupational and environmental exposures, 41–42; other medically unexplained symptoms, 39–40; overview, 25, 45; pain, 29–30, 51; pathophysiology of dysfunction, 45–46; personality changes, 60;

polytrauma, 50–51; PTSD, 32–35, 51–54; sleep disruption, 38–39, 58; substance abuse, 36–37, 56–58; summary, 42, 61; TBI, 30–32, 47–50; visible war wounds, 26–28
communication: friends and family, 116–118; Internet, 118–119; overview about, 113–114; partner, 114–116; professionals, 119–127; summary, 134
condoms, 110–111
conduct unbecoming, 16–17, 108
Connie, xiii; communication and, 116; desire phase and, 99; Gulf War illness and, 40, 59; gynecologist and, 130–131; intercourse pain and, 59; midlife and, 89; postdeployment reintegration of, 83–84; structural challenges of, 106; urinary tract infection and, 68
consent, 108
corpsmen. *See* military paraprofessionals
counselors, 120–121
cunnilingus, 5

David, xii; physiatrist and, 134; structural challenges of, 105; TBI of, 27, 47
depression, 13; baseline desire and, 54; combat deployment effects, 36, 54–55; defined, 36; Julio and, 36; Maria and, 36, 54; social impact of, 54; suicidal thoughts and, 36, 54–55; as war wound, 36
desire: brain and, 10; Connie and, 99; desire phase and, 99; Jack and, 99; Julio and, 99; Maria and, 99; normal and, 98–100; preference and, 10; senses and, 9; sexual response cycle and, 9–10, 98–100; TBI and, 47; thoughts and, 9. *See also* baseline desire
diabetes, 60
diffusion tensor imaging (DTI), 31
"don't ask, don't tell," 17
Doris, xii, 27
Doug, xiii, 89; communication and, 116; Connie's postdeployment reintegration with, 83–84
DTI. *See* diffusion tensor imaging

Edward, xii; baseline desire of, 47; physiatrist and, 134; premature ejaculation and, 103; TBI of, 27, 47
ejaculation, 11; premature, 103; retrograde, 103
endocrinologists, 132–133
environment: health and, 2; physical, 67–69
environmental exposures, 41–42
Eric, xiii; communication and, 117; premilitary experience of, 80
erogenous zones, 5

family. *See* friends and family
fatalism, 21
fellatio, 5
female: genitals, 4; reproductive organs, 4
foreplay, 5
fraternization, 16
friends and family, 116–118

gabapentin, 56
gay, lesbian, or bisexual (GLB), 17–18
gender: body structure differences, 64; hormone differences, 64–65; military service impact regarding, 66–71; overview about, 63; physical environment during deployment and, 67–69; role impact during deployment, 69–70; separation impact during deployment, 70–71; sexual trauma and, 74–77; similarities regarding, 65–66; source of difference in, 63; stigma and, 71–77; summary about, 77. *See also* female; male; men; women
genitals: development of, 6–7; female, 4; hematospermia and, 46; infertility and, 46; injuries, 46; male, 4
GLB. *See* gay, lesbian, or bisexual
Gulf War illness: combat deployment effects, 39–40, 59; Connie and, 40, 59; overview about, 59; symptoms, 40; as war wound, 39–40
gynecologists, 130–131

health: biopsychosocial approach to, 3; defined, 1; environment and, 2; nutrition and, 1–2; overview about,

1–3; social activities and, 2–3; status, 2. *See also* sexual health; *specific topic*
health care providers, 123–124
hematospermia, 46
homosexuality, 17–18
hormones: baseline desire and, 8; gender differences and, 64–65; PTSD and, 52; TBI and, 48–49, 49; testing, 49. *See also specific hormone*
hydrocodone, 37
hyperarousal, 33
hypervigilance, 33

infertility, 46
infidelity, 71; Lisa and Tom and, 71, 86; Mark and, 87; midlife and, 86–87
Internet, 118–119
interpersonal factors. *See* social and interpersonal factors

Jack, xiii; arousal phase and, 101; back surgery and, 51; before deployment, 81; desire phase and, 99; hydrocodone pills and, 37; nonconformity and, 73; numb leg of, 29–30; pain and, 51; peer pressure and, 97; primary care provider and, 125; sleep and, 38
Joe, xii; balance and, 94; baseline desire loss of, 49; climax phase and, 102; communication and, 115; endocrinologist and, 133; health care provider and, 124; TBI of, 31–32, 49; treatment sought by, 98
Jonah, xiii; baseline desire and, 96; boredom and, 100; chaplain and, 123; military paraprofessional and, 121; nonconformity and, 73; personality change of, 60, 82; sexual trauma and, 76; STD and, 105–106; on women in Marine Corps, 72
Juan, xii; arousal phase and, 101; endocrinologist and, 133; TBI of, 28, 49–50; testosterone supplementation for, 49–50
Julio, xiii; alcohol and, 37, 57; dating challenges and, 53–54; depression and, 36; desire phase and, 99; military paraprofessional and, 121–122; PTSD of, 33, 34, 35, 53–54; sleep and, 39

Laurie, xiii; gynecologist and, 131; masculine military culture and, 74; menopause and, 91; role impact during deployment for, 69; structural challenges of, 106
learning, PTSD and, 52
libido. *See* baseline desire
Lisa, xii; balance and, 94; climax and, 102–103; infidelity and, 71, 86; primary care provider and, 125; sexual health and, 81; Tom's medication and, 88; Tom's PTSD and, 53

magnetic resonance imaging (MRI), 31; mild TBI and, 48
maintenance, 11, 101
male: genitals, 4; reproductive organs, 4
Maria, xii; depression and, 36, 54; desire and, 99; loss of boyfriend, 52–53; mental health provider and, 127; PTSD of, 34–35, 52–53; sexual abuse and, 34–35; sexual response cycle and, 53; sexual trauma and, 77; sleep and, 39; treatment sought by, 98
Mark, xiii; counseling and, 120–121; infidelity and, 87; military service of, 81; as sexually adventurous, 72
marriage, military context and, 18
masculine military culture, 73–74
masturbation, 5–6
medications: adverse effects, 55–56; beta-blockers, 56; management strategies, 127–130; SSRIs, 55–56; Tom affected by, 88; tricyclic antidepressants, 56. *See also specific medication*
medics. *See* military paraprofessionals
Megan, xii; balance and, 94; climax phase and, 102; communication and, 115; endocrinologist and, 133; Joe's treatment and, 98; TBI and, 31–32
men, 22, 75–76. *See also* male
menopause, 91
menstrual cycle, 68
mental health providers, 126–127
midlife: changing health and priorities in, 85–86; Connie and, 89; infidelity and, 86–87; military service, 84–85; sexual health challenges in, 86–89; sexual health in, 84–89; Steve in, 85–86

military context and culture: conduct unbecoming and, 16–17; "don't ask, don't tell" and, 17; fraternization and, 16; GLB and, 17–18; homosexuality and, 17–18; intimate partners separation and, 23; marriage and, 18; policy and, 15–18; risky behavior and, 20–21; sex-based roles, expectations and, 19–20; sexual health affected by, 14–15, 19; sexual trauma and, 22; statistics related to, 13–14; summary, 23; UCMJ and, 15–16; women and, 17
military paraprofessionals, 121–122
military service: ages 18 to 30, 80–82; gender and, 66–71; of Mark, 81; midlife, 84–85; older veterans, 89–92; sexual health affected by, x
Monica, xiii
MRI. See magnetic resonance imaging

National Guard, 84–85
nonconformity: Jack and, 73; Jonah and, 73; to military cultural expectations, 72–74; overview about, 72–73
normal: arousal and, 100–101; balance and, 93–94; baseline desire, 96–98; climax and, 101–103; desire and, 98–100; intimate relationships, 103–104; maintenance and, 101; range of, 96–98; sexual response cycle, 98–103; summary about, 111; what is, 93–95
nutrition, 1–2

occupational and environmental exposures, 41–42
older veterans: reduced redundant capacity in, 90–91; sexual health in, 89–92
opioids, 56
orgasm, 11
oxytocin, 65

pain: combat deployment effects, 29–30, 51; Connie and, 59; Jack and, 51; musculoskeletal system and, 29–30; overview, 51; war wounds and, 29–30
pathophysiology of dysfunction, 45–46

PDE5i. See phosphodiesterase-5 inhibitors
peer pressure, 21, 97
personality changes: combat deployment effects, 60; Jonah and, 60, 82
petting, 5
phosphodiesterase-5 inhibitors (PDE5i), xiv, 129
physiatrists, 133–134
P-LI-SS-IT model, 120
polytrauma, 26; Clarissa's, 50–51; combat deployment effects, 50–51
posttraumatic stress disorder (PTSD), 13; autonomic function and, 51–52; brain and, 32–35; causes of, 52; as chronic condition, 14; combat deployment effects, 32–35, 51–54; defined, 32; dysfunctional learning and, 33–34; hormones and, 52; Julio's, 33, 34, 35, 53–54; learning and, 52; Maria's, 34–35, 52–53; overview about, 51–52; physiological markers, 34; secondary effects of, 53–54; sexual response cycle and, 53; sleep disruption and, 38; SSRIs and, 55–56; Tom's, 53; treatment of, 35
premature ejaculation, 103
primary care providers, 124–126
professionals, 119–127
promiscuity: alcohol and, 57; stimulants and, 58
prostate cancer, 60
PTSD. See posttraumatic stress disorder

redundant capacity, 90–91
reexperiencing, 33
refractory period, 11–12
reintegration, postdeployment: Connie's, 83–84; sexual health and, 83–84; sexual response cycle and, 83; Steve's, 84
relationships: normal intimate, 103–104; postdeployment reintegration and, 83–84; sexual response cycle and, 12
reproductive organs: development of, 6–7; female, 4; male, 4
retrograde ejaculation, 103
Rhonda, xiii; communication and, 118; cultural expectations and, 97; menstrual cycle and, 68; privacy

during deployment and, 67
risky behavior: binge drinking and, 21; of
Clarissa, 97; constrained opportunities
and, 20–21; fatalism and, 21; military
context and culture and, 20–21; peer
pressure and, 21; social and
interpersonal factors and, 109–111
roles: expectations and, 19–20, 88; impact
during deployment of, 69–70; Steve
and, 88
rules, knowledge of, 107–108

selective serotonin reuptake inhibitors
(SSRIs): adverse effects of, 55–56;
climax and, 102–103; overview, 55;
PTSD and, 55–56; sex and, 55; Tom
and, 55
semen, blood in. See hematospermia
senses, desire and, 9
separation impact, 23, 70–71
serotonin-norepinephrine reuptake
inhibitors, 56
sex: as personal construct, 95; therapists,
120–121; too much, 108–109
sex organs, development of, 6–7
sexual abuse, 34–35
sexual health: baseline desire and, 8–9;
decline in, 81–83; defined, 3; function
and, 3–4; importance of, 7–8; issues, ix;
Lisa and, 81; in midlife, 84–89; military
context and culture affecting, 14–15,
19; military service affecting, x; in
older veterans, 89–92; overview of
subjects presented, x–xi;
postdeployment reintegration and,
83–84; premilitary, 79–80; during
service: ages 18 to 30, 80–82; during
service: midlife, 84–85; sex drive and,
3–4; sexual response cycle and, 9–12;
short-term decline in, 82–83; social
and interpersonal factors altering,
106–111; structural challenges
redefining, 105–106; summary, 12, 92;
as taboo topic, ix–x; Tom and, 81; ups
and downs of, 79; vignettes overview,
xi–xiii; vocabulary and, 4–6. See also
specific topic
sexually transmitted disease (STD),
105–106

sexual response cycle: arousal, 10,
100–101; climax, 11, 101–103; desire,
9–10, 98–100; maintenance, 11, 101;
Maria and, 53; normal, 98–103;
overview, 9; postdeployment
reintegration and, 83; PTSD and, 53;
refractory period, 11–12; relationships
and, 12; sexual health and, 9–12
sexual trauma: gender and, 74–77; impact,
76–77; Jonah and, 76; Maria and, 77;
men and, 22, 75–76; military context,
culture and, 22; women and, 22, 74–75
short-term declines, in sexual health,
82–83
sildenafil, xiv
sleep disruption: baseline desire and, 58;
combat deployment effects, 38–39, 58;
Jack's, 38; Julio's, 39; Maria's, 39;
overview about, 58; PTSD and, 38;
substance abuse and, 39; Tom's,
38–39; as war wound, 38–39
social activities, 2–3
social and interpersonal factors: risky
behaviors, 109–111; rules, knowledge
of, 107–108; sexual health altered by,
106–111; too much sex, 108–109;
violence, 107
sodomy, 5; UMCJ and, 18
SSRIs. See selective serotonin reuptake
inhibitors
STD. See sexually transmitted disease
stereotypes, women and, 20
Steve, xiii; Agent Orange and, 42; bad
health of, 91; masculine military
culture and, 74; midlife and, 85–86;
postdeployment reintegration of, 84;
primary care provider and, 125–126;
role expectations of, 88; structural
challenges of, 106
stigma: nonconformity to military cultural
expectations, 72–74; sex-based
differential, 71–77
stimulants, 37; promiscuity and, 58
structural challenges, 105–106
substance abuse: combat deployment
effects, 36–37, 56–58; overview about,
56; sleep and, 39; stimulants and, 37;
war wounds and, 36–37. See also
specific substance

suicide, depression and, 36, 54–55
Susan, xii; David's structural challenges
    and, 105; physiatrist and, 134; TBI
    and, 47

TBI. *See* traumatic brain injury
Ted, xii; as double amputee, 27;
    hematospermia and, 46; structural
    challenges of, 105; urologist and, 132
testosterone, 65; supplementation for
    Juan, 49–50
therapists, 120–121
Tom, xii; balance and, 94; climax and,
    102–103; infidelity and, 71, 86;
    medication affecting, 88; primary care
    provider and, 125; PTSD of, 53; sexual
    health and, 81; sleep and, 38–39;
    SSRIs and, 55
traumatic brain injury (TBI): brain and,
    47–48; combat deployment effects,
    30–32, 47–50; David's, 27, 47; defined,
    30; desire and, 47; Edward's, 27, 47;
    hormones and, 48–49, 49; Joe's, 31–32,
    49; Juan's, 28, 49–50; Megan and,
    31–32; mild, 30–31, 47–48; MRI and,
    48; as signature wound, 47; Susan and,
    47; testosterone supplementation and,
    49–50; treating, 32; as war wound,
    30–32
tricyclic antidepressants, 56

UCMJ. *See* Uniform Code of Military Jus-
    tice
Uniform Code of Military Justice
    (UCMJ), 15–16; conduct unbecoming

and, 16–17, 108; sodomy and, 18
urinary tract infections, 68
urologists, 131–132

vaginal yeast infections, 68
vardenafil, xiv
veterans: treatment approach for, xiii–xiv;
    vignettes overview, xii–xiii. *See also*
    older veterans
violence, 107

war wounds: dependence from, 28;
    depression, 36; downstream effects of,
    27; examples of, 27–28; Gulf War
    illness, 39–40; invisible, 28–39;
    overview, 26; pain, 29–30; polytrauma
    and, 26; protective measures and, 26;
    sleep disruption, 38–39; substance
    abuse and, 36–37; TBI, 30–32; visible,
    26–28
women: arousal phase and, 101;
    deployment facilities and equipment
    and, 67; deployment history of, 67;
    Jonah on, 72; masculine military
    culture and, 73–74; menstrual cycle
    and, 68; military context and culture
    and, 17; role impact during
    deployment, 69–70; sex-based roles,
    expectations and, 19–20; sexual trauma
    and, 22, 74–75; stereotypes and, 20;
    urinary tract infections and, 68; vaginal
    yeast infections and, 68. *See also*
    female